Walking
In His
Promises

Money Mindset RESET
FOR THE BELIEVER

SONYA ECKEL

Walking In His Promises: Money Mindset RESET for the Believer

Copyright © 2023 by Sonya Eckel LLC

Published by Sonya Eckel LLC 1659 State Hwy 46 W, Ste 115-463 New Braunfels, TX 78132 www.walkinginhispromises.com

All rights reserved. No portion of this book may be reproduced in any form, digitally stored, or transmitted in any form or by any means - for example, electronic, photocopy, recording - without prior written permission from the publisher. For permissions contact: sonyaeckel@gmail.com.

Unless otherwise indicated, all Scripture quotations are from the Holy Bible, English Standard Version, copyright © 2001 by Crossway Bibles, a division of Good News Publishers. Used by permission. All rights reserved.

Scripture quotations marked (NIV) are taken from the Holy Bible, New International Version®, NIV®. Copyright © 1973, 1978, 1984, 2011 by Biblica, Inc.™ Used by permission of Zondervan. All rights reserved worldwide. www.zondervan.com The "NIV" and "New International Version" are trademarks registered in the United States Patent and Trademark Office by Biblica, Inc.™

Scripture quotations marked (NLT) are taken from the Holy Bible, New Living Translation, Copyright © 1996, 2004, 2015 by Tyndale House Foundation. Used by permission of Tyndale House Publishers, Inc., Carol Stream, Illinois 60188. All rights reserved.

Disclaimer *The ideas, concepts, and strategies found within are not intended to be taken as financial advice and may not be suitable for every person or situation. This work is published with the understanding that neither the author nor the publisher is held responsible for the results accrued from the ideas and concepts contained within this book. Every effort has been made to make this book as accurate as possible. However, there may be mistakes in typography or content. Also, this book provides opinions of the author and information only up to the publishing date. The author makes no guarantees concerning the level of success you may experience by following the ideas and strategies contained in this book, and you accept the risk that results will vary for each individual. The testimonials and examples provided in this book show exceptional results, which may not apply to the average reader, and are not intended to represent or guarantee that you will achieve the same or similar results.*

II Corinthians 9:6-11 (NIV)

Remember this: Whoever sows sparingly will also reap sparingly, and whoever sows generously will also reap generously. Each of you should give what you have decided in your heart to give, not reluctantly or under compulsion, for God loves a cheerful giver. And God is able to bless you abundantly, so that in all things at all times, having all that you need, you will abound in every good work. As it is written:

"They have freely scattered their gifts to the poor;
 their righteousness endures forever."

Now he who supplies seed to the sower and bread for food will also supply and increase your store of seed and will enlarge the harvest of your righteousness. You will be enriched in every way so that you can be generous on every occasion, and through us your generosity will result in thanksgiving to God.

Dedication

To Jake, Luke, Benji, and Sam. The four of you are precious gifts from God, and I am beyond blessed to be your mother. I know that God is doing amazing things in each of your lives and has an incredible calling for each of you. I pray God's blessings over you, that you may walk in His might and wisdom all the days of your life! I am so proud of you!

And to my hubby of over 22 years! Willie, I am beyond blessed to have you as my life partner on this incredible ride. You love the Lord and bless others with the gifts He has given you! Thank you for giving and loving so generously. I love you!

Contents

Introduction ix

The Correct Order in our Walk with God 1

Scriptural Basis for God's Abundance and Provision 13

Identifying Faulty Mindsets and Beliefs. 23

Reset to God's Truth 41

Become a Generous Giver and Grateful Receiver 51

Finding the Dream Within You. 61

ACTION Time. 77

Appendix A 89

Appendix B 97

About the Author. 103

Introduction

Have you ever felt like it's impossible to achieve financial breakthrough despite doing all the "right" things? Does it feel like your financial goals are evading you?

Welcome to this Money Mindset RESET! As we go on this journey together, I want to remind you that this book is written from my Christian perspective. If talking about wealth or finances in combination with the Bible makes you uneasy, no worries. I was there myself—until God began showing me the INCREDIBLE promises in His Word! This book is based on my personal journey with God helping me grow in so many areas over the past 20 years. Your journey will not look exactly like mine, but we can glean from one another's experiences!

There have been times in my life when finances were tight and I was praying, asking God to show me a way to add income. Lack of finances has placed unnecessary strain on many marriages and relationships. I discovered that I highly dislike financial stress! Can you relate? Yet, I was conflicted, wondering if financial freedom was God's will for me. But God has taken me on a journey through His Word, showing His incredible LOVE for His children, and His desire to bless them!

As you work through this book and the accompanying scriptures, my hope is that you will see that YOU are designed for growth and success. Do you realize that God does NOT intend for you to live in lack, scarcity, or poverty? We serve God of the breakthrough, God of abundance, Creator of all things, and God of His Word! Would you like to learn how to believe for and live in His glorious promises?

Dear Friend, you are not here by accident! I believe God wants to show you more of Him: His provision, promises, and truth.

In building a home-based business, God showed me I would need to grow my financial mindset to continue growing my business and income. Perhaps you also sense that you need to grow in your money mindset to achieve your goals. In the early years of my business, as someone who loved Jesus with all my heart, I still carried some faulty, non-biblical beliefs around money.

God has led me on a path, showing me many amazing things in His Word. I am not a biblically trained scholar, nor a financial expert. I am still His work in progress, growing and learning every day. Throughout my journey, I have often been asked if I can recommend a biblically aligned mindset book, as many are more secular in nature. Again, this book is written from my own personal learning and experiences so far in life. I am deeply grateful for the many, many mentors God has put in my life. God has taken me on a deep dive into my favorite book of all time, the Bible, with the Holy Spirit as my guide.

Honestly, for many years of my Christian journey, I would not have said the Bible was my favorite book because I had a very limited understanding of it. Although I loved Jesus and had grown up reading it, I read it with a set of "glasses" of preconceived ideas and beliefs. I read it more because I thought I "should" than to truly get to know God through His Word. Perhaps you can relate. But 2010, the Lord led me to study Revelation and then Daniel (both books which had greatly intimidated me). This began my deeper searching of the scriptures and my love for His Word.

Then, in 2018, while on a camping trip, we received the devastating call that my baby brother had died by suicide. To say it rocked my world with a grief I had never known would be a huge understatement. I had never experienced that depth of pain and loss in my life. As I laid there, my body racking with sobs, I felt the Holy Spirit put Romans 8:28 on my heart. I was so mad! I replied, "Lord, how could you EVER work something like this for good?" Three months later, I received the call that my mother had died in a car accident. At this point, I remember my heart going completely numb. I was not sure how to move through the intense grief and loss.

In the midst of the pain, I found comfort by immersing myself in the Bible, starting in Genesis and reading it cover to cover. Through the intense hurt, God was there beside me, drawing me closer to Him. Life on Planet Earth is not always free from pain and heartache. I share this to say that God works all things together, even the toughest experiences in our life, to bring us closer to Him. It was through this time of grief and healing that the Bible became my favorite book of all time!

In my time in direct sales, I have had people say, "Sonya, you should write a book." I would often respond, "If God ever gives me a book to write, I will write it." And so, here we are. I pray it will be a blessing to you on your journey. I also pray that it will cause you to dive deeper into God's Word! He has given me many verses, but truthfully, He shows me more every day! His Word is so infinite and alive! This book only scratches the surface of understanding God's plans and desires for us! May it be a springboard into so much more fullness and abundant life in Him!

Throughout the book, when I mention money or finances, many of us will think in terms of our country's money system. "Money" includes resources and exchange of value, including things like the barter system of goods and services. But wealth and riches come in varied forms, and with God, it goes far beyond just financial blessing and increase. Having the abundant life in Christ means far more than just financial assets. God's biblical principles stay consistent no matter the specific form of wealth.

"Wealth" can look different to each person and is relative to each person's specific situation and location. In addition to the spiritual riches of eternal salvation and the fruit of the Spirit, such as love, joy, and peace, most of us have a mental idea of what "riches" means in the natural sense. For instance, when I think of God's financial blessings, I think of walking in the provision and blessings of our Heavenly Father, with overflow to be able to give generously in every situation. Your definition may be different, and that is okay! In fact, you may be opening this book with a rather negative feeling about "riches" or "wealth" in the natural sense. I have been there, as well.

For years, I read the Bible from a "spiritual only" viewpoint. I did not feel the Bible was relating as much to things in our natural, earthly realm—especially money—but rather speaking mostly to our eternal life. Many of us hesitate to talk too much about finances for fear of making money a god in our life. We never want to make the blessings of God an idol!

God has shown me how His principles work opposite of how we have been trained to think in this natural realm. For instance, in Proverbs 11:24: "One gives freely, yet grows all the richer; another withholds what he should give, and only suffers want." This biblical concept flies in the face of conventional advice that to get ahead, money and resources must be saved, or even hoarded. But that approach is not what the Bible tells us. In God's plan, we are not just the recipient of resources, but rather we are His children with His Spirit within us, living as His conduit of resources. For much of my life, I thought of finances regarding our own family being provided for, but I now feel God challenging me to think in terms of having "extra", above just our own family's needs, so that we can always give generously.

Most of us were ushered into the world with a set of 'glasses' handed to us. These glasses were most likely intended to protect us. They impact the way we see the world. In our early years, these 'glasses' may have been composed of religion, traditions, beliefs, culture, words spoken over us, or things done to us or for us.

Several years ago, I prayed, "Father God, take off my 'glasses.' Remove my preconceived notions and beliefs and teach me Your truth." I wanted to see Him in complete truth (Psalm 145:18-20) without the "tinting" of the beliefs I had either been given or had adopted along my life journey. He has certainly been faithful in answering that prayer!

I often think of the scripture in Luke 11:7 and Matthew 7:7, where Jesus reminds us that those who ask will receive. James 4 says that we do not have because we do not ask, and reminds us to ask with righteous motives and humility, seeking God's purposes first, according to His Spirit within us . Throughout this journey together, I encourage you to be bold and specific in asking the Lord for help with all things in your life (including finances) and to keep your heart, mind, and arms open to receive from Him. He is the God of all abundance! If you would like to join me in seeking truth in His Word, you can start with this prayer:

> **Father God, thank You for bringing me into this journey of discovering Your truth and abundance. I ask that You lift off the "glasses" of my previous beliefs that may be tinting or distorting Your perfect truth. Lead me into Your truth. Your Word tells me the Holy Spirit will teach me all things, and I step into this journey trusting You. In Jesus' name I pray.**

Before you write this off as some "prosperity doctrine" book, let me say this book is not about God being our magic genie or wealth being some "special formula". This is not about making everyone who reads this book a billionaire. No, this book is firstly about our relationship with Jesus Christ and loving God with all our heart, mind, soul, and strength. In John 15 (NIV), Jesus talks about abiding in Him, the vine, and bearing much fruit. He says, "If you remain in me and my words remain in you, ask whatever you wish, and it will be done for you. This is to my Father's glory, that you bear much fruit, showing yourselves to be my disciples." Consequently, He gives us the ability to walk in His truth, promises, overflowing provision, and blessing, according to His Word and for His glory!

Are you ready? Have your Bible handy as we go on this journey together!

Jesus said in John 10:10, "The thief comes only to steal and kill and destroy. I came that they may have life and have it abundantly." Jesus came to give us abundant life! Paul writes in Ephesians 3:20-21, "Now to him who is able to do far more abundantly than all that we ask or think, according to the power at work within us, to him be glory in the church and in Christ Jesus throughout all generations, forever and ever. Amen."

> **JOHN 10:10**
>
> The thief comes only to steal and kill and destroy. I came that they may have life and have it abundantly.

Throughout this book, I include some sample prayers. For each one, first read it silently to yourself. If it is a prayer you feel led to pray, I encourage you to speak it out from your heart to God. If you are in a place where you can say the prayer aloud, the spoken word is powerful. I hope you will read to the end. If you only read select parts, you may miss a scripture or promise God has for you. Open your hands and heart to receive all that He has for you! And, for those of you who prefer not to write in the book itself, you will find a notes page you can download to complete the written exercises at **http://RequestWorkbook.WalkingInHisPromises.com/**.

Abundant Blessings,

Sonya Eckel

R-E-S-E-T

REST IN HIM
EQUIP YOURSELF WITH HIS WORD
SET YOUR EYES ON JESUS
EXPECT HIS PROMISES TO BE YES & AMEN
TAKE THE DAILY ACTIONS HE GIVES YOU

The Correct Order in our Walk with God

MODULE ONE:
THE CORRECT ORDER IN OUR WALK WITH GOD.

As Christians, many of us have beliefs we **think** are biblical, yet, with a deeper look at the scriptures, we may find we have believed (and lived by) partial truths or lies. I was raised in a Christian home, reading the Bible, for which I am very grateful. In reading the Bible, however, I found myself "cherry-picking" verses to support my preconceived mindsets and beliefs. God has instructed me to read books and letters in the Bible in their entirety before grabbing random verses to support my cause or belief system, as well as to ask the Holy Spirit's guidance as I read. This is what I try to do, and I encourage you to do the same. Again, keep your Bible handy as we move forward.

I invite you to join me in looking beyond our preconceived notions and taught beliefs. Let's investigate the one guaranteed source of truth, God's Word.

As we go through all these things together, keep in mind Matthew 6, where Jesus tells His disciples they cannot serve God and money. He also tells them not to be anxious about their life. "Therefore do not be anxious, saying, 'What shall we eat?' or 'What shall we drink?' or 'What shall we wear?' For the Gentiles seek after all these things, and your heavenly Father knows that you need them

> **MATTHEW 6:33**
>
> But seek first the kingdom of God and his righteousness, and all these things will be added to you.

all. But seek first the kingdom of God and his righteousness, and all these things will be added to you" (Matthew 6:33).

When I see the word "all" in scripture, I "capitalize" it in my brain to remind myself that with God, all means ALL! (As you read the scriptures, I encourage you to highlight the word "all" when you see it!).

In our spiritual walk, the ORDER of things is critical. In all things, put God first, with Jesus as our Lord and Savior. In the power of the Holy Spirit, we seek to live in His righteous will. By putting Him first in our heart, His Word tells us we can then live and walk in His freedom and blessing.

How do we know that we love God with all our heart? Romans 5:5 says, "and hope does not put us to shame, because God's love has been poured into our hearts through the Holy Spirit who has been given to us." Through faith in Jesus, God gives us His Holy Spirit and pours His love into us. I John 4:19 reminds us that we love God because He first loved us! When we love the Lord, we seek His will before our own and we obey His commandments. In I John 5:3, John writes, "For this is the love of God, that we keep his commandments. And his commandments are not burdensome."

His Word tells us when we seek first His kingdom and righteousness, all these other things will also be provided. The Bible gives us specific instructions on how to live and walk with God (an easy place to start is with the book of Proverbs). In Romans 1:25, Paul writes we must worship God, the Creator, rather than worshipping His creation. Yet, as God's beloved children, we do get to enjoy and praise Him for His incredible creation and blessings! In Romans 2:7-11 (NIV), it says, "To those who by persistence in doing good seek glory, honor and immortality, he will give eternal life. But for those who are self-seeking and who reject the truth and follow evil, there will be wrath and anger. There will be trouble and distress for every human being who does evil: first for the Jew, then for the Gentile; but glory, honor and peace for everyone who does good: first for the Jew, then for the Gentile. For God does not show favoritism."

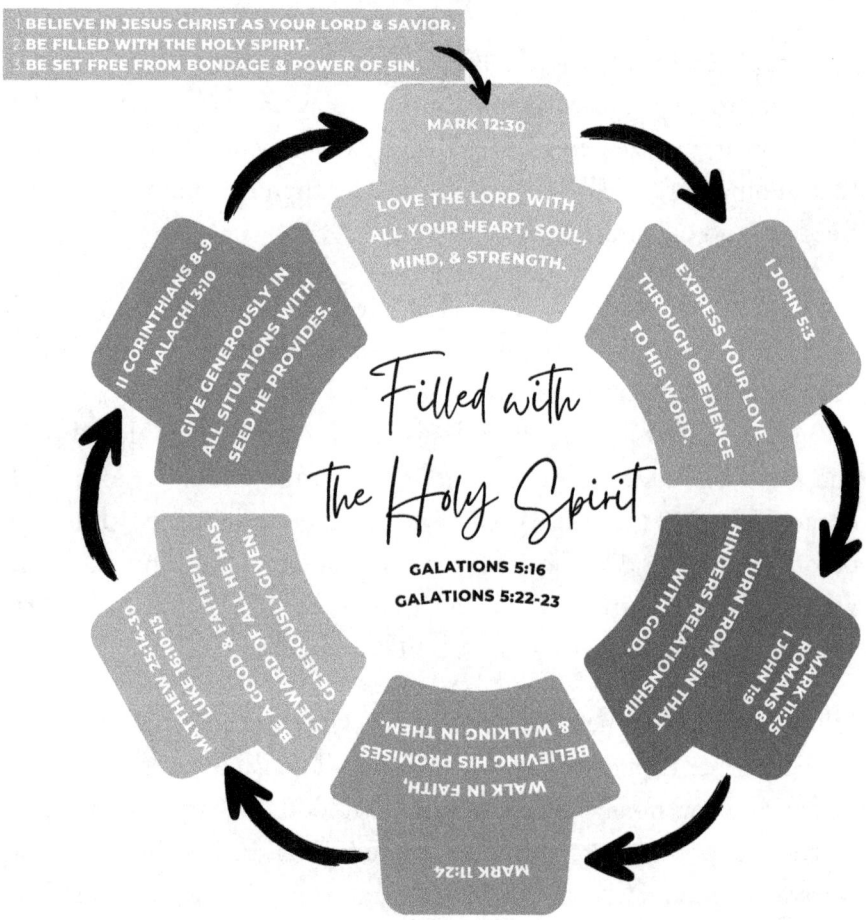

God told Solomon in II Chronicles 1:11-12 that because Solomon asked for wisdom and knowledge, not wealth, possessions, or honor,

He would also give him wealth, possessions, and honor. He rewarded Solomon for having things in the proper order. And David knew the importance of what was in his heart when he wrote Psalm 139 and asked God to search his inmost heart to see if there was any grievous way in him.

I Timothy 6:10 (NIV) tells us, "For the love of money is a root of all kinds of evils." Unfortunately, many people have misquoted this verse, stating instead that money is the root of all evil. If you have carried that belief, go back, and re-read the verse. Much of scripture is dedicated to money and how God uses it for His purposes and glory.

The reason the love of money is the root of many evils is that it moves money into God's space, as a god or idol in our life. Therefore, the correct order is that we love God with all our heart, soul, mind, and strength (Mark 12:30) first!

MARK 12:30

And you shall love the Lord your God with all your heart and with all your soul and with all your mind and with all your strength.

In I Timothy 6:17-19 (NIV), Paul writes, "Command those who are rich in this present world not to be arrogant nor to put their hope in wealth, which is so uncertain, but to put their hope in God, who richly provides us with everything for our enjoyment. Command them to do good, to be rich in good deeds, and to be generous and willing to share. In this way they will lay up treasure for themselves as a firm foundation for the coming age, so that they may take hold of the life that is truly life." In this book, I am talking about our money mindset from a Christian perspective but know this: our spiritual wealth always comes first. Then, as we read God's Word, we can see that He also desires to bless us naturally.

We see in scripture that we are not to be greedy or consumed with love for money or material possessions. We also see that God desires to bless His children with resources, finances, and increase so they can be a blessing to many others. In Matthew 25, Jesus shares the parable about the talents that the master gave to his servants. Being a wise steward of the master's resources and multiplying the talents were rewarded. In Luke 16:10-12 (NIV), after sharing the parable about a dishonest manager, Jesus then said, "Whoever can be trusted with very little can also be trusted with much, and whoever is dishonest with very little will also be dishonest with much. So if you have not been trustworthy in handling worldly wealth, who will trust you with true riches? And if you have not been trustworthy with someone else's property, who will give you property of your own?"

Our calling is to be trustworthy stewards of the resources, tools, blessings, and money the Lord gives us. We are not to serve the idol of money! Therefore, a biblical money mindset RESET considers that we FIRST love God with all our heart, mind, soul, and strength.

We must know that God is GOOD. When we face difficult things, we remember that it is the **enemy** who comes to steal, kill, and destroy. Those things are NOT from God. John 8:24 says that our enemy, the devil, is a liar and the father of lies. When Satan deceived Eve and Adam into sin, and sin separated them from God, it left a broken world. But God, fulfilling the Abrahamic covenant, brought Jesus to pay the penalty for sin and redeem all of mankind. God gives us free choice, so it is up to us to accept the paid-in-full gift of salvation in Jesus. James 1:17 says, "Every good gift and every perfect gift is from above, coming down from the Father of lights, with whom there is no variation or shadow due to change."

The Bible tells us that we, as believers, will face persecution (II Timothy 3:12, John 15:18, Matthew 5:11, Matthew 5:44, Romans 12:14). We will be faced with temptations common to man. But we have the strength, through the Holy Spirit dwelling in us, to be overcomers instead of our previous condition of being a slave to sin. Even Paul, in II Corinthians 12, when he was faced with a "thorn in the flesh", a messenger of Satan, God promised that His grace was enough to deal with it. So, whatever or whoever this messenger of Satan was, God assured Paul that His grace was sufficient to deal with it, even if not removed. Paul celebrated that he, in his human weakness, was able to walk in the power of Jesus. This book is about walking in the power of the Holy Spirit, not our own human strength.

Sometimes the question is asked, **"Is it godly and righteous to EXPECT blessing from the Lord**?" Romans 2:9-11 tells us that there **are** expected results from things we do. Paul writes that glory, honor, and peace come to everyone who does good, including Jews and non-Jews, for God shows no partiality or favoritism. Throughout scripture, God gives clear examples of what pleases Him and what brings blessing. **Yes, we can expect blessing, goodness, and love** to follow us all the days of our life because we are in Jesus and have received the Holy Spirit within us! Romans 3:23-26 tells us that God justifies, or makes right, those who have faith in Jesus. So, we are righteous and favored in His sight!

I believe the enemy of our soul would like us to believe God is inconsistent and unpredictable. The enemy would like for us to attribute atrocities and pain to God. He would like us to believe that God randomly hand-picks those He chooses to bless. Statements or questions like "Who can know the heart of God?", "Why does God allow such bad things to happen to good people?", or "God sends rain to the just and unjust" are often used to argue the idea that God will sovereignly choose to do whatever He chooses to do, regardless of a person's effort, generosity, or righteousness.

While bad things do happen to good people here on Earth, it is the enemy of our soul who comes to steal, kill, and destroy. Just as Satan rebelled against God, he desires to deceive people to also rebel against God. God, in His sovereign wisdom, saw fit to give humans free will, and He does not go back on His Word. The Bible and history show that the heart of man, without God, is not inherently good (Jeremiah 17:9-10). God, on the other hand, is good (Psalm 34:8, John 3:16-17), shows mercy on the just and the unjust (Matthew 5:45, Romans 11:32, Titus 3:5, James 1:17), and desires that all would be saved (I Timothy 2:3-4). God's Word tells us He wants to be in relationship with us; He wants to be a Father to us (John 1:12, II Corinthians 6:18, Galatians 3:26). To be in relationship with God means that we can get to know the heart of God, in fact, He lays it out in His scriptures (Ephesians 1:17, I John 2:3, I John 4:16). In Jesus, we are born-again as a new creation with the Holy Spirit dwelling in us (II Corinthians 5:17, I Peter 1:23).

In I Corinthians 2:11, Paul tells us that the Spirit of God knows the thoughts of God. And we know that as believers, God's Holy Spirit comes to dwell in us. Paul tells us in Ephesians 1:9 that God has made known to us (believers in Jesus) the mystery of His will by His good pleasure, purposed in Jesus, and Jesus said in Mark 4:11 that the secret of the kingdom of God has been given to believers. We must understand that God is GOOD, He is a God of order, and that He desires that ALL will be saved through the blood of His Son, Jesus! He does not desire that ANY should perish (II Peter 3:9

and I Timothy 2:4)! Hebrews 11:6 tells us that to please God, we must believe He exists **and that He rewards those who diligently seek Him**. (It is important to specify that eternal salvation is NOT works-based but by faith in Jesus Christ alone, so that none may boast (Ephesians 2:9). However, scripture shows us that God loves to reward those who walk with Him in love and faith.)

I John 3:22-23 tells us, "and whatever we ask we receive from him, because we keep his commandments and do what pleases him. And this is his commandment, that we believe in the name of his Son Jesus Christ and love one another, just as he has commanded us." And in I John 5:13-15 (NIV), "I write these things to you who believe in the name of the Son of God so that you may know that you have eternal life. And this is the confidence we have in approaching God: that if we ask anything according to his will, he hears us. And if we know that he hears us—whatever we ask—we know that we have what we asked of him."

In these verses, John is writing that when we receive what we ask for, it is because we believe in Jesus, keep His commandments, and do what pleases Him. The Holy Spirit in us changes our heart and causes us to want to do His will!

God's divine order:

1. Accepting, believing in, and confessing Jesus as our Lord and Savior.
2. God placing His Holy Spirit within us.
3. Our hearts changing to desire to fulfill the commandment of believing in Jesus and showing His love to one another.
4. Living in God's promises written in His Word and walking within His scriptural principles.

BEFORE WE MOVE ON, I REALIZE THAT THIS PORTION WILL NOT APPLY TO ALL OF YOU, BUT I DO NOT WANT TO MAKE ANY ASSUMPTIONS.

Perhaps you choose to live by Christian values but have never actually accepted Jesus as your Lord and Savior. He offers us the gift of salvation and adoption through grace alone! If you have not yet accepted Jesus as your Lord and Savior, I invite you to make this your moment of saying yes to Him!

Why, you ask?

First, it is the most incredible, life-changing decision you will ever make! According to Romans 3:23-25, we "all have sinned and fall short of the glory of God, and are justified by his grace as a gift, through the redemption that is in Christ Jesus, whom God put forward as a propitiation by his blood, to be received by faith." Only Jesus can make us perfectly righteous before God. Romans 6:23 says, "For the wages of sin is death, but the free gift of God is eternal life in Christ Jesus our Lord." In Christ, our sin has been paid IN FULL! We simply need to accept His gift! Romans 10:9-10 tells us, "because, if you confess with your mouth that Jesus is Lord and believe in your heart that God raised him from the dead, you will be saved. For with the heart one believes and is justified, and with the mouth one confesses and is saved."

Secondly, what I share in this book hinges on walking in the power and authority of the Holy Spirit. The Holy Spirit comes to dwell in us when we accept Jesus as our Savior who died to cover the penalty of ALL our sins. Having Christ in us and us in Christ brings God's supernatural blessing into our lives. Once we are born again into the body of Jesus Christ, His promises apply. This is not to say that believers in Jesus will not face challenges, hardships, and persecution, but in Christ alone, we get to partake in God's promises.

If you want to accept Jesus as your Lord and Savior, you can say this simple prayer from your heart to receive His gift of salvation and grace!

> **Father God, I'm not perfect. But I believe that Your Son, Jesus Christ, died for me. I believe His blood washes me clean to the point that You remember my mistakes no more! Save me. Change me. I give You my life. Jesus, I make You my Lord and Savior! I joyfully receive the gift of the Holy Spirit!**

If you prayed this prayer for the first time, welcome to God's family! Not only have you received the gift of eternity with God, but you also receive His Holy Spirit IN you and become a son or daughter of the Most High God!

Romans 5:1-2 says, "Therefore, since we have been justified by faith, we have peace with God through our Lord Jesus Christ. Through him we have also obtained access by faith into this grace in which we stand, and we rejoice in hope of the glory of God." And Romans 5:5, "and hope does not put us to shame, because God's love has

ROMANS 5:1-2

Therefore, since we have been justified by faith, we have peace with God through our Lord Jesus Christ. Through him we have also obtained access by faith into this grace in which we stand, and we rejoice in hope of the glory of God.

been poured into our hearts through the Holy Spirit who has been given to us."

Hallelujah!! Let's take a moment to raise our hands and praise the Lord! He loves you so much! Tell Him how much you love Him!!! Praise Him because he is WORTHY of praise! Even when we do not "feel" like praising Him, we can choose to praise! Praise is a powerful weapon that can turn around difficult situations of all kinds! Love, praise, and gratitude to God provide a strong foundation on which to build your life and your finances. (If you just made the decision to accept Jesus as your Lord and Savior, message me! I want to celebrate the BEST decision of your life with you!)

Scriptural Basis for God's Abundance and Provision

MODULE TWO: SCRIPTURAL BASIS FOR GOD'S ABUNDANCE AND PROVISION.

In my younger years, I largely linked my identity to the opinions and approval of others, which were societal "norms." I never felt good enough, pretty enough, smart enough, athletic enough. You get the idea. As a believer, I did not realize my true identity: a daughter of God!

As a result of living under a mistaken identity, I sometimes spoke unkindly to myself. God has blessed me with a deep love for others, so I would not have said such unkind things to them, yet I told these things to myself. And because I had been repeating these "scripts" for years, I did not even realize I was saying them. Thankfully, God did not leave me there.

Several years ago, God laid this question on my heart: How did He, the Creator of the universe, create it? I answered that He spoke it into existence (Genesis 1). Genesis 1:26-27 tells us that God created man in His image and gave them dominion over all the earth. The Lord helped me understand, "I, the Lord, created you in my image! I made you beautifully and for a purpose. And if I created the world by speaking it into existence, I have also given YOU the power to create with your words. Steward them wisely." He then brought me to Psalm 139:14, "I praise you, for I am fearfully and wonderfully made. Wonderful are your works; my soul knows it very well."

This conversation with God changed me. It was a pivotal point when I decided to stop speaking negatively about myself and how He made me. It made me realize the creative power in my words and that my words DO CREATE. For better or for worse, what I speak out IS creative!! So then, I had to dig deeper. What did I want to create with my words? I knew I wanted to create goodness and blessing in my life and the lives of others.

Yes, if it is true that we are created in God's image, then our words hold incredible creative power. Let me ask you a question. If someone were recording your words and you were to listen back, what would you hear yourself speaking (as well as thinking or speaking silently to yourself) on an average day? **What are you creating, whether intentionally or unintentionally, in your life and the lives around you?** Are you speaking goodness and blessing? Or are you unintentionally speaking curses over yourself and others?

Ephesians 5:1-2 says, "Imitate God, therefore, in everything you do, because you are his dear children. Live a life filled with love, following the example of Christ. He loved us and offered himself as a sacrifice for us, a pleasing aroma to God." God speaks blessing and we are called to do the same. You can bless or curse with your words. As imitators of God, we can choose to bless others.

Luke 6:45 tells us that out of the abundance of our heart, our mouth speaks. Proverbs 18:21 says death and life are in the power of the tongue. Philippians 4:8 reminds us to think on things that are true, honorable, just, pure, lovely, commendable, excellent, and worthy of praise. When we are born-again, we are no longer a slave to sin (Romans 6), but rather, God has given us the gift of free will, meaning we get to choose what we think and speak.

In my early years walking with Jesus, I found myself coming to God as a beggar, praying that He would find *something* in me that would be pleasing to Him. Later in my journey, He revealed the fullness of GRACE to me, showing me that IN Jesus, I am His beloved child. He began showing me that I am to walk confidently as His daughter, a CHILD of the Most High God, but in a spirit of humility, knowing it is nothing of myself or my own works, but solely through the blood of my Lord and Savior, Jesus.

One of the first steps in resetting your financial mindset is knowing your identity in Christ Jesus (Romans 8:14-17)! YOU are a child of God! Romans 11:17 tells us we, as believers, are grafted into God's promises to share in the nourishing root of Israel, in Christ. So, IN Christ Jesus, we become Father God's son or daughter. In II Corinthians 6:18, Paul refers to II Samuel 7:14, saying, "And I will be a father to you, and you shall be sons and daughters to me, says the Lord Almighty." John writes in John 1:12, "But to all who did receive him, who believed in his name, he gave the right to become children of God." Galatians 3:26-29 (NIV) says, "So in Christ Jesus you are all children of God through faith, for all of you who were baptized into Christ have clothed yourselves with Christ. There is neither Jew nor Gentile, neither slave nor free, nor is there male and female, for you are all one in Christ Jesus. If you belong to Christ, then you are Abraham's seed, and heirs according to the promise."

> **ROMANS 8:14-17**
>
> For all who are led by the Spirit of God are sons of God. For you did not receive the spirit of slavery to fall back into fear, but you have received the Spirit of adoption as sons, by whom we cry, "Abba! Father!" The Spirit himself bears witness with our spirit that we are children of God, and if children, then heirs—heirs of God and fellow heirs with Christ, provided we suffer with him in order that we may also be glorified with him.

I John 3:1 says, "See what kind of love the Father has given to us, that we should be called children of God; and so we are." I encourage you to make a study of all the places in the Bible where God assures us we are HIS children!

Imagine that! You are a daughter or son of the Most High God, the Creator of all things. As we study scripture, we see God extends all His benefits, including forgiveness, redemption, abounding provision, and healing. He crowns us with love, tender mercy, and the gift of faith, filling our life with good things and renewing our youth like eagles! Wow! What promises He gives us! Read Psalm 103 and underline the words that speak most deeply to your heart.

As heirs and children of God, Jesus transferred to us what is His. John 16:15 says, "All that the Father has is mine; therefore I said that he will take what is mine and declare it to you." We, God's children, have access to His abundant riches. With Jesus as your Lord and Savior, you become a child of God. Read Paul's prayer in Colossians 1:9-14,

> And so, from the day we heard, we have not ceased to pray for you, asking that you may be filled with the knowledge of his will in all spiritual wisdom and understanding, so as to walk in a manner worthy of the Lord, fully pleasing to him: bearing fruit in every good work and increasing in the knowledge of God; being strengthened with all power, according to his glorious might, for all endurance and patience with joy; giving thanks to the Father, who has qualified you to share in the inheritance of the saints in light. He has delivered us from the domain of darkness and transferred us to the kingdom of his beloved Son, in whom we have redemption, the forgiveness of sins.

Read that again. We are qualified to walk in His power since we have been transferred from the enemy's domain into the kingdom of the Son. Imagine the power of praying this each day!

> Thank You, Father God, for filling me with the knowledge of Your will through the wisdom and understanding that the Holy Spirit gives. Help me to live a life pleasing to You in every way! Help me bear fruit in every good work, growing in my knowledge of You, and being strengthened with ALL power according to Your glorious might! You, Father, have qualified me to share in the inheritance of Your people in the kingdom of light. Thank you for rescuing me from the domain of darkness and bringing me into the kingdom of Your Son, in whom I have redemption!

In II Corinthians 8:9 Paul writes, "For you know the grace of our Lord Jesus Christ, that though he was rich, yet for your sake he became poor, so that you by his poverty might become rich." This is the "great exchange" that has given us privileges as children of God and citizens of heaven (Ephesians 2:11-22)! As citizens of heaven, we need to understand what the Bible tells us about our rights as believers in Christ Jesus! Matthew records this in Matthew 7:11: "If you then, who are evil, know how to give good gifts to your children, how much more will your Father who is in heaven give good things to those who ask him!"

As a believer, the Spirit of Him who raised Jesus from the dead dwells in YOU (Romans 8:11). Romans 8:31-32 tells us, "If God is for us, who can be against us? He who did not spare his own Son but gave him up for us all, how will he not also with him graciously give us all things?"

ROMANS 8:31-32
What then shall we say to these things? If God is for us, who can be against us? He who did not spare his own Son but gave him up for us all, how will he not also with him graciously give us all things?

In Romans 8:37, Paul writes, "No, in all things we are more than conquerors through him who loved us." Romans 8:17 says, "and if children, then heirs—heirs of God, and fellow heirs with Christ." And in Philippians 4:19 (NIV), Paul writes, "And my God will meet all your needs according to the riches of his glory in Christ Jesus."

Do you believe God wants His children to walk in lack and poverty? Are you feeling that He is the God of lack or poverty? No, He is a good, good Father who is the giver of all good gifts (James 1:13-17), who loves to bless His children! Do you believe to your core that God is good? Do you trust God?

I ask this question because there was a day when I loved God but believed that He would probably ask me to do the things I really did not want to do. I was not completely convinced He had my best interest in mind. In fact, I was afraid to give Him full control, because I did not fully trust Him. But as I have grown to know Him better, I trust Him with every cell in my body! I know He is good! He is completely trustworthy to fulfill His promises.

II Peter 1:3-11 shares a powerful message.

> His divine power has granted to us all things that pertain to life and godliness, through the knowledge of him who called us to his own glory and excellence, by which he has granted to us his precious and very great promises, so that through them you may become partakers of the divine nature, having escaped from the corruption that is in the world because of sinful desire. For this very reason, make every effort to supplement your faith with virtue, and virtue with knowledge, and knowledge with self-control, and self-control with steadfastness, and steadfastness with

> godliness, and godliness with brotherly affection, and brotherly affection with love. For if these qualities are yours and are increasing, they keep you from being ineffective or unfruitful in the knowledge of our Lord Jesus Christ. For whoever lacks these qualities is so nearsighted that he is blind, having forgotten that he was cleansed from his former sins. Therefore, brothers, be all the more diligent to confirm your calling and election, for if you practice these qualities you will never fall. For in this way there will be richly provided for you an entrance into the eternal kingdom of our Lord and Savior Jesus Christ.

When I read this, I notice that "has granted" is in past tense. It has already been done. I see He has given us ALL things that pertain to life and godliness. Yes, this includes eternal life in heaven, but Peter is writing to those who have obtained faith equal to his own through Jesus, so these verses are not about an unbeliever receiving eternal salvation. Rather, Peter is wanting them to know their privilege in walking within God's divine power and promises, escaping from the broken world system. "Eternal" means there is no start or end. The "eternal kingdom of our Lord and Savior Jesus Christ" reminds us that there is no start or end to His kingdom. We know God (Father, Son, and Holy Spirit) has always existed. So, Jesus has always been and will always be the king of this eternal kingdom. Scripture tells us that one day, Jesus will come to reign physically here on Earth during the millennial reign, but eternally, He is king.

In the New Testament, there are many promises and stories of God's goodness to us! Pore over them and receive what God offers! There are amazing promises found in the Old Testament, as well! Invite the Holy Spirit to continue showing you more and more!

There is much debate over whether Old Testament blessings and promises apply only to Israel or if they also apply to the Church. Romans 11 tells us that we, Gentile believers, are grafted into the root of Israel because we are IN CHRIST JESUS. Galatians 3:14 (NIV) says, "He redeemed us in order that the blessing given to Abraham might come to the Gentiles through Christ Jesus, so that by faith we might receive the promise of the Spirit." And Romans 11:29 tells us the gifts and calling of God are irrevocable. In II Corinthians 1:19-22, we see that all promises of God find their "Yes" in Jesus. It says,

> **2 CORINTHIANS 1:19-22**
> For the Son of God, Jesus Christ, whom we proclaimed among you, Silvanus and Timothy and I, was not Yes and No, but in him it is always Yes. For all the promises of God find their Yes in him. That is why it is through him that we utter our Amen to God for his glory. And it is God who establishes us with you in Christ, and has anointed us, and who has also put his seal on us and given us his Spirit in our hearts as a guarantee.

> For the Son of God, Jesus Christ, whom we proclaimed among you, Silvanus and Timothy and I, was not Yes and No, but in him it is always Yes. For all the promises of God find their Yes in him. That is why it is through him that we utter our Amen to God for his glory. And it is God who establishes us with you in Christ, and has anointed us, and who has also put his seal on us and given us his Spirit in our hearts as a guarantee.

In Hebrews 8:6 (NLT), it says "But now Jesus, our High Priest, has been given a ministry that is far superior to the old priesthood, for he is the one who mediates for us a far better covenant with God, based on better promises."

Considering these passages, I encourage you to read through the promises in Deuteronomy 28:1-12. Moses shares how God desires to bless Israel if they walk in His statutes. The difference between then and now is GRACE, or "better promises." We, as believers, are IN Christ Jesus! In the Old Testament, it was "yes" when they obeyed and stayed faithful to God, and "no" when they strayed.

As Christians, we are no longer slaves under the old law. God has now covered His part AND our part (because we are IN JESUS and grafted into His righteousness, even though we humanly do not walk perfectly). Have you ever seen a product or website with the words "Powered by…"? God gave me the understanding that we can walk in His promises BECAUSE we are powered by His Holy Spirit!

IN CHRIST JESUS, all of God's promises are "yes." In Jesus, we become heirs to the promises! Hallelujah! How He loves us! Are you walking in His promises? Are you saying "yes" to receiving what God offers you? Are you getting the importance of knowing and walking in your identity in Christ?

Before we move forward, I encourage you to proclaim these truths:

"I am a child of the Most High God, in whom He is well pleased."

"In Christ Jesus, I unlock the mysteries and blessings of all God has intended for me!"

You might ask, "How can God be pleased with me?? I've messed up so many times!"

Remember, when God looks at you and me through the blood of Jesus, who paid the penalty of our sin (past, present, and future) IN FULL, He sees us only as His beloved child. Abiding in Christ, the Holy Spirit empowers us to live a life that bears much fruit for Him. John 15 tells us the power of abiding in Him.

Identifying Faulty Mindsets and Beliefs

MODULE THREE: IDENTIFYING FAULTY MINDSETS AND BELIEFS ABOUT MONEY.

I am insanely grateful for my farm upbringing and the fact that my parents and grandparents loved Jesus and sought to raise us in alignment with biblical values. With that said, in my youth, I picked up some interesting thoughts about money; honestly, some were not helpful or biblically true.

If you know a farmer, at least an old-school farmer, you will be hard-pressed to find exactly how many acres of land they farm, how many head of livestock they have, or their net worth. Why? Because it is considered taboo to talk about things related to money or wealth. And there is a certain appeal to that approach. To this day, I tend to be very private about such things, also.

In the good farming years, very little was mentioned about money, and those felt like low-stress times. But what made the most profound impact on my 'little girl heart' was the tough years. The years where lack was felt and spoken, and the stress was palpable.

"Farming is tough!" "We can't afford that." "We don't have the money."

And I remember the heated arguments my parents had around money. (And in talking with others, this was not unique to my parents' relationship!) In my young heart and mind, money became associated with stress, guilt, shame, and regret more than with positive experiences.

I also picked up a belief that "rich people" were proud and not very godly, both of which I did not want to become. Beliefs such as these, that money would demean our character or cause us to be proud, arrogant, or mean, can keep us from receiving and walking in God's promises. I also had the idea that contentment is godly, so by default, I assumed it was ungodly to want "more." This meant, in my mind, gratitude and contentment could not easily coexist with a desire for growth and increase.

I blame no one for these beliefs. They were simply something I had acquired and needed to work through. Likely, each of us has some similar beliefs to work through, assess, and decide whether or not to keep. Thankfully, God has shown me it brings Him JOY to see His children GROW; it brings Him JOY to give to and bless His children! Ask, and you shall receive. Seek, and you shall find (Luke 11:10).

What about always having a grateful heart (Colossians 3:15-17)? YES, definitely! We build our lives on a foundation of gratitude for all Jesus has done for us and generosity with our resources for His purposes. Then, we believe for His overflowing provision! (Remember God's correct order from Module 1!)

How about you? Do you have some beliefs popping up? Here is a prayer to ask God to reveal any lies or partial truths you've been believing and to replace them with His truth.

> Father God, thank You for walking with me on this journey to find Your truth about me, my family, my finances, and my life. I thank You that You care about the details of my life. I ask that You reveal all beliefs that I am carrying that are not of You. Bring them to the surface in Your beautiful, healing light so we can remove these faulty beliefs and lies and replace them with Your truth about my identity in You and Your love and abundance. In Jesus' name I pray.

Earlier in my life, before I realized how MUCH God cares about our finances, I felt led to start a home-based direct-selling business. I found despite how much I despised financial stress and burden, I was still trying to function with faulty beliefs and toxic emotions around money.

Our inner thoughts and beliefs are what create the emotions we feel. Most times, our beliefs and thoughts FEEL so real and so true. Walking out life under mistaken beliefs (that we 100% believe to be true) can make the journey more difficult. I was attempting to build a business with an unhealthy, unbiblical money belief system. But God is so faithful to guide and grow us in Him! The changes in my thinking did not happen overnight; rather it has been an ongoing process and continual conversation with God.

My direct-selling company provided a way to add income that fit my core values and purpose, which was an immense blessing. As I earned that first $500, then $2000 per month, and eventually replaced what I had made as a full-time physical therapist, I felt beyond blessed. In operating my "little business," I found myself thinking, "Who needs more than this per month?"

I specifically felt the Lord ask me, "Do you want your team to also earn this much per month?" My answer was, "Yes, Lord! Absolutely!" And then I felt Him kindly say, "Then you need to be willing to receive more."

It was that simple. I had decided no one in their right mind needed more than this amount per month, and in the process of this "contentment," I was not willing to receive what God wanted to pour out in my life and in the lives of my team members. He showed me if I wanted others to experience this same blessing, I would need to learn how to receive more.

RECEIVING His abundance instead of letting my sense of unworthiness limit His gifts and learning to walk worthy through the blood of Jesus have been a huge part of my journey.

> **Heavenly Father, thank You for revealing the enemy's lies about me and lies I have believed. I thank You that I can walk worthy IN CHRIST JESUS! Help me know victory and live from victory because I am Your child, in whom You are well pleased! Help me receive ALL You have and desire for me! I ask You to remove any faulty beliefs from every cell of my body and replace them now with Your truth!**

As we move forward, I want to remind us that living the abundant life Jesus promised in John 10:10 means far more than just finances. In fact, there are many wealthy people who lack joy, peace, purpose, or satisfaction. Worldly wealth without spiritual wealth is disappointing and empty. Living the abundant life in Christ is all-encompassing. God's way is not man's way (Isaiah 55). Jesus says in Matthew 19:26 that with man these things are impossible, but with God, all things are possible. God's blessings work counter to how our human nature thinks. Proverbs 10:22 says, "The blessing of the LORD makes rich, and he adds no sorrow with it." What a sweet promise to walk in! As I shifted my mindset and leaned into God's leading, He has done immeasurably more than I could have wished or imagined (Ephesians 3:20)!

Beliefs can be rather sneaky. Often, we do not realize they even are there because they are embedded in our subconscious, the part of our brain that basically runs our life. But you know who knows every single faulty subconscious belief within you? You guessed it! Your Heavenly Father! And He loves when we seek Him, to help us uncover and release these unhealthy, unproductive, and often untrue, beliefs.

I'll give you an example. When I was coming up on my 40th birthday, I did not want to say aloud that I was 40. I didn't care that I was turning another year older, but somehow "40" was causing me some angst. I had never previously felt that way about birthdays, and my husband called me out on it. He said he thought it was a bit crazy that I wouldn't just say I was turning 40. And he was right. It was odd.

So, I began to seek the Lord about it, and He brought up some beliefs that I had carried since I was a young girl. Some of my mother's best friends were my heroes; I really looked up to them. Suddenly, God brought back to my memory some conversations I had listened in on as a child. Things like, "Everything falls apart after 40!" or "After 40, the pounds started packing on around the middle!" came back into my awareness. The interesting thing was that when I turned 40, I began gaining weight (prior to uncovering these subconscious beliefs).

So, I had some belief work to do. Through prayer and taking off the "glasses" of those inner beliefs, I began noticing that many women in their 40's, 50's, 60's and beyond who were trim, healthy, and fit! I realized that I was buying into a belief system that was impacting my life in an undesirable way. And then I asked God to clear out those old beliefs that had been lurking under the surface for so many years. Interestingly, these belief systems did not rear their head until they became relevant in my life. Similarly, God had to show me old money beliefs that I had picked up along my life journey. For each thing He uncovered and revealed to me, I sought His help in removing it.

Our experiences can create certain beliefs. Then, our beliefs create our experiences. And unfortunately, sometimes the beliefs we have accepted as "truth" are not true. Have you ever believed a lie and later found out it was not true? How did that belief impact your journey? When we believe lies, we miss out on experiencing the full blessings God desires to pour out. God continually brings me back to His source of absolute truth, the Word of God. In this module, I want you to become aware of any negative thoughts, faulty beliefs, and unhealthy emotions you carry, specifically around money and finances.

Does just talking about money make you anxious? Do you believe there is never enough money to go around? When you think of money, do you think of debt and lack? Do you think of hardships caused by families fighting over money? Have you experienced broken relationships caused by money issues? What comes to your mind? Identifying these feelings will be crucial in your Money Mindset RESET.

TIME TO IMPLEMENT!

Please take a break in your reading to DO this exercise.

1. Ask God for His guidance throughout this Money Mindset RESET journey. Invite Him to reveal what is in your heart and help you heal the lies and partial truths and replace them with His perfect, complete truth. As believers in Jesus, we can come to Him with ANYTHING and EVERYTHING. He cares about YOU and the small details of your life, as well as the "big spiritual things." As His child, we have a relationship with our heavenly "Daddy" by talking with Him about everything!

2. Here is a simple prayer: "Dear Heavenly Father, I love You! I know the enemy has planted lies and partial truths, but what he meant for harm, You will work together for good. I ask You to reveal these beliefs, bringing them to the surface in your beautiful light, and help me release them forever, replacing them with Your truth."
3. Write down the thoughts and emotions rising up as we talk about money. I am serious. Take a break and DO this exercise. You may be surprised by what comes to the surface if you give it space. Now, do not worry! We are not going to keep these things. But we are going to identify them so we can ask the Lord to take them and replace them with His truth!

_____

_____

_____

_____

_____

OK, welcome back! Now that you have taken time to write down your money stories, beliefs, and possibly even traumas, I am going to give you some examples of beliefs I have uncovered in myself or in coaching others.

As you read through these, checkmark the ones that resonate with you. If you're not sure, ask the Holy Spirit if this is something you carry. Some of these came on board at a very young age, and we may not even be sure why we believe them to be true. But we do. And it is time to deal with them under the power and authority of Jesus.

This list is not all-inclusive, but a starting point to get you thinking about what types of money beliefs and preconceived notions you have bought into as "truth." Bring them before the Lord to discern if they are His truth.

"Finances are always tight."
"I don't know how to make money."
"I never have enough."
"We can't afford that."
"I always lose."
"I can never get ahead."
"I can't seem to catch a break."
"I never win."
"I can't make ends meet."
"I am broke."
"I always get the short end of the stick."
"No one likes me."
"I don't have any friends."
"No one ever listens to me."
"Money is the root of all evil."
"Money ruins relationships."
"Wealthy people are greedy."
"The rich are the problem in our world."
"Money doesn't grow on trees."
"Wealthy people are bad."
"Money destroys people."
"It is not safe to be rich."
"If I make more money, I'll have to pay too much in taxes."

"If I'm wealthy, I will be at risk."
"It's dangerous to be rich."
"Money causes problems."
"God is a harsh God more than a loving God who blesses."
"If I become rich, I will become selfish."
"If I am making more, it means I'm taking it from someone else."
"God is using poverty in my life to grow my character."
"God loves poor people more than rich people."
"God doesn't like rich people because He said it is difficult for them to get into heaven."
"You have to have money to make money."
"I don't have time to make more money."
"I am unworthy."
"I am not a good money manager."
"I am not good with money."
"I do not want to have the responsibility of having money."
"I am afraid of what money will bring out in me."
"I will have to be dishonest to get rich."
"Rich people got there by stepping on others."
"There's not enough money for that."
"The only way to get rich is to save."
"Money doesn't come easy."
"What will others think of me?"
"Will people just like me for my money?"
"Who am I to ask anything of the Most High God?"
"Shouldn't I just be grateful and content with all that He has already given?"
"I should not want more money because contentment is godly."

When I first did this exercise, I found I carried many false and faulty beliefs. Here is the GREAT news! God is faithful to remove **what you are willing to give up**.

I am super thankful for my husband, Willie, who helped me put a healthier face to money. He showed me how we could use it to bless others by giving and making an impact for good. He helped me see the vision of land for our boys to enjoy. Money is a fantastic tool and resource God desires to give us to care for our family, church, city, and the world around us.

If you were to put a face to money and ask how it could be a BLESSING in your life and the lives of those around you, what comes up? Better relationships? Less arguments? Lack of finances can cause unnecessary stress and put pressure on relationships. Could you say "yes" to more memories, experiences, generosity, travel, events, or activities?

You can start this process by saying, "Wouldn't it be amazing if…" and start filling in the ways that money could be a blessing in your life and in the lives around you. Then, take a minute to write these things down.

_____

_____

_____

_____

_____

II Corinthians 9:10-11 says, "He who supplies seed to the sower and bread for food will supply and multiply your seed for sowing and increase the harvest of your righteousness. You will be enriched in every way to be generous in every way, which through us will produce thanksgiving to God."

We will talk more about these verses in our giving and receiving module, but **can you imagine being so blessed to be able to say YES to being generous in every way?!** That is what God wants for you as His child! I have learned God wants not only to cover all the needs of me and my family, but He also wants to give His children even more resources and "seed" so we can sow generously whenever and wherever He leads us (II Corinthians 8-9)!

Along with limiting core beliefs, we can also carry unhealthy, detrimental EMOTIONS regarding money and finances. Thoughts are different from emotions, but thoughts and beliefs often lead to a certain feeling. For instance, if I believe I am overwhelmed, it may lead to an emotion of despair. If I believe I am horrible at something, it may lead to an emotion of embarrassment. The Bible tells us to take ALL thoughts captive (II Corinthians 10:5). When we continue to feed unhealthy, untrue beliefs and thoughts, they grow into emotions in your heart and being.

Proverbs 4:23-24 reminds us to guard our heart, for out of it flows our actions. Romans 12:2 reminds us that we are to be transformed in the renewal of our mind. And Philippians 4:8 reminds us to think on things that are TRUE. So biblically speaking, thoughts in our mind and emotions in our heart ultimately guide our actions and results.

TIME TO IMPLEMENT!

Take a minute to put a name to the feelings you experience when you think about money (or the lack thereof) or anything indirectly related to finances. Write down whatever emotion is coming into your awareness. No judgment; just write. It could be any emotion, but some common ones are anxiety, fear, dread, or frustration.

If you need some help getting started, think about the most stressful money-related situation(s) in your life and allow the feelings about it to rise to the surface.

Bring these emotions into God's beautiful light so that together with Him, you can deal with them once and for all!

_____

_____

_____

_____

_____

I am proud of you for taking the time to be vulnerable and give these emotions a face and space. Once lies and toxic emotions are brought into God's light, they already have less power over us because we recognize them as a tool of the enemy to steal, kill, destroy, and keep us from our God-given destiny. This is the first step in becoming free from their impact and control over our lives.

Next, look through this list. Again, this list is not exhaustive but includes other emotions someone may feel when talking about anything directly or indirectly associated with money. Are there any on the list you also feel but did not think to write down? Go ahead and add them to your list. And then let me share how I learned God doesn't intend us to carry these anymore!

- Abandoned
- Aching
- Anger
- Annoyed
- Anxious
- Apathetic
- Betrayed
- Bitterness
- Blame
- Cheated
- Confusion
- Controlled
- Deceived
- Defensive
- Depression
- Desperation
- Discouragement
- Disgust
- Distressed
- Dread
- Embarrassment
- Failure
- Fatigue
- Fear
- Frustration
- Furious
- Grief
- Guilt
- Hatred
- Heartbroken
- Helpless
- Hopeless
- Horrified
- Humiliated
- Indecisive
- Insecure
- Jealous
- Loss
- Manipulated
- Misunderstood
- Nervous
- Overwhelm
- Panic
- Peeved
- Pride
- Regret
- Rejection
- Resentment
- Sadness
- Shame
- Sorrow
- Stubbornness
- Unsupported
- Unworthy
- Vulnerability
- Worry
- Worthlessness

Just as you can partner with God to remove faulty beliefs, you can ask God to remove negative, paralyzing, limiting emotions! Are you ready to live without these limiting emotions and belief systems? Yes?! Are you ready to be FREE from the power these have held over you? OK, let's do this!! There is FREEDOM in Christ! Freedom from slavery to sin's power in our life.

In faith, bring each emotion to God and ASK Him to remove it, and He WILL. For instance, if you discovered you carry a feeling of anger, you could start by praying a prayer like this:

> **Lord, please remove anger from me completely in Jesus' name! No matter if it is a generational emotion, an emotion that stems from a trauma, or no matter the cause, I ask that You search and shine Your loving light on every cell of my body, every part of my soul, and REMOVE anger completely. Wherever it was lodged, flood those places with Your perfect love and joy! Heal any wounds or scars in my soul caused by anger. In Jesus' mighty name!**

That's right. Ask in faith and **believe that you have received**. Mark 11:24 says, "Therefore I tell you, whatever you ask in prayer, believe that you have received it, and it will be yours." It really is that easy! This literally TRANSFORMED my life. When I learned I did not have to be a slave to my emotions anymore, and God would remove the harmful emotions when I asked, the FREEDOM was incredible!

For me, it happened quite quickly. When I realized it was **my choice** to give up these emotions and faulty beliefs and that God would willingly, supernaturally remove them from me, I was completely floored by the results. Without all the baggage, it was like God was transforming every cell in my body. The associated hurt, unforgiveness, and pain began to disappear so much that I couldn't "feel" it or even recall it the way I had before. God was dissolving the power these emotions had held over my life. Incredible. I encourage you to seek His supernatural provision and help in this area!

Remember, this is not a "magic formula." It is being in relationship with your Heavenly Father who HEALS and RESTORES because He loves you and it is His will for you to no longer live in bondage!

Let me be very honest, though; He revealed some things I had been carrying for quite a while. Some feelings I felt very JUSTIFIED in carrying, and sometimes, it was not easy to give them up. They had, in essence, become part of me.

For instance, I remember when I discovered I was carrying a strong emotion of betrayal. I felt someone had betrayed my confidence by sharing something that I considered very private. In talking with God in this process, I was literally weeping, not wanting to give it up. I felt justified in feeling betrayed. I felt justified in holding it against this person. I also had a belief that if I kept it, I could prevent betrayal from happening to me again. Then I felt the Holy Spirit say, "You can keep it if you want. Or you can give it to me and be free. Are you ready to set it down? Are you ready to let it go?"

While weeping, I prayed, "Lord, take it! I don't want to walk with this burden anymore." And immediately, it was completely gone. Just like that. And then I wept in absolute gratitude. Again, I was blown away by the FREEDOM and LIGHTNESS I felt. If you also experience this response in healing and removing old and unwanted baggage, emotions, and thoughts, I encourage you to step out in faith and say "yes" to the Lord! He bore our burdens on the cross. Friend, you do not need to carry the load anymore. You are a NEW creation in Christ!

In releasing these limiting emotions, God gave me this vision: He showed me the toxic emotions I was choosing to carry were holding me back, as if I were running on a road with a parachute strapped on my back, resisting my forward movement and energy. As I was running, I could not figure out why it felt SO HARD. He showed me emotions could be like that. They can drag you down, exhaust you, and impair you from fulfilling your God-given calling.

But then, He showed me the proverbial latches on the front of the parachute vest. If I chose, I could unbuckle those, and let the parachute crumple down on the road behind me, powerless to create further resistance in my journey. He has taught me to walk in His freedom according to Galatians 5:1.

But it was my choice to make. Would I choose to lay down those emotions at His feet? The writer of Hebrews in chapter 12 encourages us, "let us also lay aside every weight, and sin which clings so closely, and let us run with endurance the race that is set before us." And Paul writes in Philippians 4:6 we are to not be anxious about anything. God did not design us to carry these heavy burdens. Jesus says in Matthew 11:28, "Come to me, all who labor and are heavy laden, and I will give you rest."

We can leave our baggage and our traumas at the feet of Jesus (Matthew 15:30). For certain emotions and associated traumas, my human pride wanted to say "no" to laying them down. My inner "protector" wanted to say no. My inner self believed holding on to those emotions would somehow protect me from it happening again. Often, we hold on to beliefs or emotions with the idea they will protect us. But IN CHRIST, we no longer must captain our boat. We are no longer our sole protector. We are COVERED, tucked under the wings of the Most High!!! Read Psalm 91 (I have included it at the close of this book). As you read it, take note of the word WILL.

Perhaps you've come through extreme poverty and lack in your life. A person can easily shift into a poverty mindset, believing in lack, scarcity, catastrophe, and "waiting for the other shoe to fall." These beliefs can limit what God desires to do in us, for us, and through us. This could hold you back from financial breakthrough! I encourage you to ask God to take these faulty beliefs and throw them into the depths of the sea! To walk in the abundant, blessed life that Jesus purchased for you and me, He invites us to relinquish these emotions and past traumas. **In faith, simply ask Him to remove each one**. He will do it.

As you clear out this past baggage, continue declaring His truth over yourself. Do not go back and feed the trauma, the limiting belief, or the emotion ever again. Instead, intentionally choose to walk in your identity as a child of God. Whenever you are tempted to go back to such a belief or emotion, intentionally speak blessing and His truth and promises over yourself.

If you're unsure what to say, start with, "I am a child of the Most High God in whom He is well pleased!"

The enemy of our soul does not want us to know our true identity in Christ. He does not want us to know our rights as a citizen of heaven and a child of God. Affirm your identity in Christ often. Embrace it fully. Walk in His promises.

Reset to God's Truth

MODULE FOUR: RESET TO GOD'S TRUTH.

God does not force our hand. He has given us free will. So, asking Him to remove these things is a conscious decision we get to make! There is FREEDOM in it! Saying "yes" to His offer to remove these things can move you toward living a life of abundant blessing: the life Jesus purchased for you when he died on the cross and rose again, triumphant over sin and death!

Are you ready and willing to permanently let go of unhelpful, unhealthy beliefs and emotions? Are you ready to live victorious in Christ?!

As a quick refresher on what we covered earlier, we must **seek FIRST the kingdom of God and His righteousness, and all else we need will be added**. The Bible speaks strongly against allowing the love of money to become a god or idol in our life! God's word tells us the LOVE of money is the root of many evils. The love of money means worshipping it instead of our Creator. The key is to love God with all our heart, mind, soul, and strength, and all of those things will be added to you (Matthew 6:31-33)!

The question to ask ourselves is, "Do I seek first the kingdom of God and His righteousness before every other thing?" If so, then all these things shall be added to you because that is what Jesus says. We know God is a covenant-keeper and always faithful to His Word. There are no lies in Him!

One of the BEST ways to reset to His truth is to post His Word throughout your home. Speak it over you, your loved ones, and every aspect of your life! To get you started, I would like to gift you some printable scriptures. You can find them at http://PrintableScripture.WalkingInHisPromises.com/.

As we reset our money mindset, it is vital to realize money is not good or bad. Rather, money is simply a tool or resource. Money does magnify what is in your heart. Thankfully, as a believer, God has given you a new heart. He has transformed you so when you have blessings, you will have a heart to use them to glorify God. In the Bible, Jesus talks much of finances, increase, bearing fruit, and being a good steward (Matthew 25:14-30). He wants us to abound because we are ABIDING in Him (II Corinthians 9:8).

As born-again children of God, we can utilize resources, such as money, to shine God's light throughout the world. To bring blessings, God desires that His people have resources. The Holy Spirit in us causes us to be good stewards of all He has given us.

Going back to faulty beliefs about money, let's say, for example, you marked the statement, "Finances are always tight." How do you move past a belief that you have perhaps lived with all your life? Perhaps you were raised in poverty and scarcity. Maybe you have gone through completely devastating financial times. How do you let go of something that you have "seen confirmed again and again" in your past? Perhaps friends and family in your life are continually affirming the lie you have believed. How do you move forward into a future that does not need to look like your past? How do you move into living the abundant life Jesus talked about?

First, recognize that although you may have experienced tight finances in the past, that is not the reality God wants for you. He does not wish for His beloved children to live in lack, scarcity, or pain. **Remember this biblical truth:** It is the thief who comes to steal, kill, and destroy, but **Jesus** came to give us life, and life ABUNDANT (John 10:10)!

As we have covered earlier, the abundant life in Jesus is gained through our relationship with Him. His Holy Spirit in us produces the fruit of the Spirit of love, joy, peace, forbearance, kindness, goodness, faithfulness, gentleness, and self-control. The abundant life includes being on mission for the Lord, living in your calling and purpose, having beautiful relationships with others, and is much more than just possessions and financial assets. With that said, much of the Bible is also dedicated to finances, and since this is a Money Mindset RESET book for the Believer, let's talk about how to reset our financial beliefs to align with His Word.

You may be thinking all these things are simply too good to be true. You might be saying, "Sonya, but you do not know MY story!" And if you are thinking in a natural sense, you are right; this might all seem "too easy" and perhaps downright impossible! Remember what Jesus said in Matthew 19:26! With God all things are possible… even the things that are impossible in our human ability. And remember what Jesus said in Matthew 7:7, "Ask and it will be given to you; seek and you will find; knock and the door will be opened to you."

One of the reasons I have included a large amount of scripture in this book is because faith and belief are key to receiving God's promises! Romans 10:17 tells us, "So faith comes from hearing, and hearing through the word of Christ." If faith comes from hearing the Word of God, to grow in your faith, you will want to read and listen to God's

Word often. Faith grows as you realize God is a God of His Word, He cannot lie, and His promises are real and true for you!

And remember, in Ephesians 6, Paul tells us to put on the armor of God to help us stand against the enemy's attack. This includes the belt of **truth**, breastplate of **righteousness**, readiness of the **gospel** of peace, shield of **faith**, helmet of **salvation**, and the "**sword of the Spirit, which is the Word of God**". This helps us walk in the supernatural power of the Lord instead of walking in our own strength. And then Paul reminds us to, "pray in the Spirit on all occasions with all kinds of prayers and requests." Truly, God's Word is a lamp to our feet, a manual for living the abundant life!

If you are ready to move into God's reality for your life instead of believing that finances are always tight for you, simply ask God to remove this belief from your inner being, from your subconscious wiring, and from every cell of your body. We can ask Him to clear it completely from our mind, body, and soul, along with healing any scars or wounds associated with it. Then, ask Him to replace it with His truth found in His Word.

> **Lord, write these truths on my heart where the faulty beliefs and lies have been removed. You are the God of great reversals. Thank You for clearing out these lies and replacing them now with Your truth! I pray this in the mighty name of Jesus! Amen.**

God is abundant above anything we can think or imagine (Ephesians 3:14-21). He is our Heavenly Father who wants to bless us. Ephesians 1:3 says, "Blessed be the God and Father of our Lord Jesus Christ, who has blessed us **in Christ** with every spiritual blessing in the heavenly places." He invites us into heavenly places, through relationship with Him, even as we walk here on Earth.

TIME TO IMPLEMENT!

Take some time to declare these scripture-based statements over your life and the lives of your family members and loved ones. You can also print them and display them in your home (i.e., bathroom mirrors, office areas, framed pictures, etc.)

It is God's pleasure to give His children more than what we can even think or imagine. (Ephesians 3:14-21)

God is pouring out blessings in my life. (Isaiah 44:3, Psalm 20:4)

God shows me my path and each step of the way because I am His child. (Psalm 119)

He is a lamp to my path. (Psalm 119:105)

He goes before me and hems me in from behind. (Psalm 139:5)

He prepares my way, and He has my back. (Isaiah 52:12)

God supplies my every need according to His unfathomable riches. (Philippians 4:19)

My cup overflows with His goodness. (Psalm 23)

He is a good, good Father. (James 1:16-18)

He provides above what I can ask or imagine! (Ephesians 3:20-21)

I am a citizen of heaven and live under Father God's righteousness and jurisdiction. (Philippians 3:20)

He is faithful to hear and answer my prayers. (I John 5:14)

I am a child of God! (John 1:12)

There is no lack in God's kingdom, and I am a daughter/son of God! (Psalm 23:1, Psalm 34:9-10)

I walk in His promises, power, and ability to steward the resources He gives me. (II Peter 1:4)

He uses me as a conduit of His abundance to bless many. (II Corinthians 8-9)

God loves to bless His children to bring Himself glory. (Romans 11:36, I Corinthians 10:31)

I receive God's abundant blessing with open arms and a grateful heart! (Mark 11:24)

I am blessed. (John 3:16, Ephesians 2:8, Psalm 1:1-6)

When we speak God's Word back to Him and over ourselves, our loved ones, and our situations, it is powerful. Speak BLESSING over you, your family, your finances, and your future. God cares about all these things! There are many sample blessings in the Bible you can pattern this after, for instance, Aaron's blessing (Numbers 6:22-26) and the Prayer of Jabez (I Chronicles 4:10).

> **The Lord bless you and keep you;
> the Lord make his face to shine upon you and be gracious to you;
> the Lord lift up his countenance upon you and give you peace.**

One of the keys to living in the freedom of the Lord is to STOP speaking curses over ourselves or our families. When you are tempted to proclaim negative things, choose instead to speak a blessing.

> **Jabez called upon the God of Israel, saying, "Oh that you would bless me and enlarge my border, and that your hand might be with me, and that you would keep me from harm so that it might not bring me pain!" And God granted what he asked.**

In your money mindset journey, immerse yourself in His Word! Speak His promises over you, your family, and others. God is eager to save, forgive, prosper, heal, and bless. We, as believers, need to understand these things about Him! If we do not, it would be difficult to believe in faith for them! If we do not believe His promises and miracles are for us today, we can miss out on so much! By speaking out promises from His Word over our life, we are giving Him place, space, and opportunity to say "yes" and do those things!

As you read on, I want you to experience God's blessing and abundance in EVERY area of your life, not just finances! If we, in Christ Jesus, are grafted into God's promises, there is great power in reading these scriptures aloud.

Become a Generous Giver and Grateful Receiver

MODULE FIVE:
BECOME A GENEROUS GIVER AND GRATEFUL RECEIVER OF GOD'S BLESSINGS.

To give is a blessing. In fact, in God's Word, giving is something that comes with many benefits. The Bible tells us giving is even more blessed than receiving. In Acts 20:35, Paul writes, "In all things I have shown you that by working hard in this way we must help the weak and remember the words of the Lord Jesus, how he himself said, 'It is more blessed to give than to receive.'" We want to grow in generous, cheerful giving, as God's Word tells us. God-centered giving is a key part of our Money Mindset RESET.

Proverbs 3:9-10 says, "Honor the Lord with your wealth and with the firstfruits of all your produce; then your barns will be filled with plenty." So, we can choose to walk in a generous, abundant mindset. In Luke 6:38, Jesus says to "give, and it will be given to you. Good measure, pressed down, shaken together, running over, will be put into your lap. For with the measure you use it will be measured back to you."

> **PROVERBS 3:9-10**
>
> Honor the Lord with your wealth and with the firstfruits of all your produce; then your barns will be filled with plenty, and your vats will be bursting with wine.

Malachi 3:10, referring to tithing, says, "Bring the full tithe into the storehouse, that there may be food in my house. And thereby put me to the test, says the LORD of hosts, if I will not open the windows of heaven for you and pour down for you a blessing until there is no more need." In Malachi 3:11 (NIV), the Lord says, "I will prevent pests from devouring your crops, and the vines in your fields will not drop their fruit before it is ripe." God desires to provide for, protect, and bless you. He wants to be generous to us. He is just waiting for us to step into our true identity in Christ and walk in His statutes. Hebrews 13:16 says, "Do not neglect to do good and to share what you have, for such sacrifices are pleasing to God." If you are trying to figure out how to start giving, start by giving where you can, even if it does not feel like much. Serve and give with the skills, gifts, time, and resources God has given you.

To increase in our desire and ability to give, we can simply ask the Lord to fill us with His Spirit, His heart, and His generosity. I invite you to pray this prayer with me.

> **Dear Lord, I ask that You put in me a generous heart that matches Your heart! You have been so, so good to me, and I know You delight in Your children who are generous conduits of Your blessings and abundance to others. Lord, help me be able to give generously in all situations and on all occasions as Your Word says. Let me always be a cheerful giver! Lord, thank You for giving me seed to plant, resources to give, and abundance with which to bless others and shine Your light! To You be the glory!**

What if you set aside a certain percentage of what you earn to give to your church? In addition to money, there are many other ways to also be generous.

For example, do you have the gift of hospitality? Gift of administration? Gift of leadership? Gift of serving? Gift of teaching? God will utilize the gifts He has given us to bring about blessing and breakthrough for others. Pray about how you are to use your gifts.

Paul wrote to the Corinthians about giving (II Corinthians 9:6-15 NIV):

> Remember this: Whoever sows sparingly will also reap sparingly, and whoever sows generously will also reap generously. Each of you should give what you have decided in your heart to give, not reluctantly or under compulsion, for God loves a cheerful giver. And God is able to bless you abundantly, so that in all things at all times, having all that you need, you will abound in every good work. As it is written: 'They have freely scattered their gifts to the poor; their righteousness endures forever.' Now he who supplies seed to the sower and bread for food will also supply and increase your store of seed and will enlarge the harvest of your righteousness. You will be enriched in every way so that you can be generous on every occasion, and through us your generosity will result in thanksgiving to God. This service that you perform is not only supplying the needs of the Lord's people but is also overflowing in many expressions of thanks to God. Because of the service by which you have proved yourselves, others will praise God for the obedience that accompanies your confession of the gospel of Christ, and for your generosity in sharing with them and with everyone else. And in their prayers for you their hearts will go out to you, because of the surpassing grace God has given you. Thanks be to God for his indescribable gift!

I have read this scripture many times. At first, I spiritualized it to think about the seed being spiritual righteousness, or maybe something to do with the salvation of others. But I did not stop long enough to consider what Paul was really writing about.

Clearly, he was talking about generous giving. Consider if the "seed" he mentions is our money and resources. It says that God gives seed to the sower, or the one who sows. By giving generously, we plant the "seed" under God's authority and for His use. This chapter clearly outlines how God intends for finances to work! The return is exponential.

There was a time when I began to seek God about finances, that I found myself primarily praying about provision for our own family and those close to me. God has shown me that I should be thinking far beyond abundant provision for only "my people". He wants us to abound and be able to give generously where and when He leads.

Having grown up on a farm, I am familiar with the power of a seed. When you plant one kernel of wheat, God CREATED that one seed to sprout and grow into a plant. The plant then creates MANY heads of wheat, simply because ONE kernel was planted. That is the power of multiplication. When the farmer invests and plants his seed, he has faith it will grow, because that is how God created seeds. He does not need to sit alongside his field and beg the seeds to grow. Jesus uses the analogy of the seed in Mark 4:27, saying how the seed sprouts and grows even when we do not understand exactly how.

Paul's analogy of a "seed" helps us understand how God intends for His people to utilize our finances. Planting "seed" into God's purposes leads to the scriptural promise of the "harvest", being enriched in EVERY way, above and beyond just having our own needs met! Imagine walking in overflow, being able to GENEROUSLY give on EVERY occasion!!!

The ruler of this world, the devil, wants us stressed, trapped, broken, sick, and locked into his debt-based system (Proverbs 22:7). The

Bible tells us that we are in the midst of a spiritual battle. In John 12 and again in John 16, Jesus refers to the "ruler of this world", but He makes it clear that the devil is "cast out" and "judged". So, because of Jesus' victory, we no longer need to live as slaves to the enemy's system. Instead, we, as God's children, must learn to walk in God's economy instead of the world's debt-based economy.

God desires His kids to give freely, which will create thanksgiving, even in the hearts of those who do not yet believe. These verses say that God supplies the seed to us. We plant the seed (the giving of our money and resources) in faith, under His inspiration and jurisdiction. When we plant the seed He has given us, His Word tells us He will enlarge our harvest. The Lord gives the increase. When we have knowledge of His promises and accept them as true, we joyfully plant seeds for His purposes! His returns are above anything we could imagine. His promise is to not only meet our needs but to give a generous return and bless many, allowing us to be abundantly generous in all situations!!

Where are you being called to sow your money right now? Ask the Holy Spirit to put it on your heart, and then be ready with your "Yes, Lord!" Even if you do not feel you have anything to give, I encourage you to step out in faith and sow what you can. When you plant in faith, believe for a multiplied harvest because that is what His Word tells us. He is a generous God and loves to bless.

"Faith" is a word we often hear in our Christian walk. Let's take a minute to look at what the Bible says about it. Hebrews 11:1 tells us faith is the ASSURANCE of things hoped for, the CONVICTION of things not seen. In Romans 4:21, Paul writes that Abraham was FULLY CONVINCED God was able to do what He had promised! When we sow seed into God's purposes, we can be CONFIDENT in faith that He is trustworthy to fulfill His promises! Faith is being in agreement with what GOD says in His Word.

So often, we tend to come into agreement with others instead of with God's Word. Studying and speaking His Word over your life, circumstances, and finances aligns you with Him! Hebrews 11:6 says, "And without faith it is impossible to please him, for whoever would draw near to God must believe that he exists and that he rewards those who seek him." In Mark 9:23, the father of a boy with a mute spirit says to Jesus, "if you can do anything" and Jesus responded, **"'If you can'! All things are possible for one who believes.**" In this passage, Jesus was correcting his disciples for their lack of faith and the boy's father for questioning "if Jesus could". There are places in the Bible where Jesus commends someone for his or her faith, and there are other places where He chides for lack of faith and belief. I encourage you to make a study of these situations, and the result of faith versus unbelief.

Faith and fear do not co-exist. Recently, the Holy Spirit drew my attention to Mark 4:40, where Jesus had just calmed the sea. He said to his disciples, "Why are you so afraid? Have you still no faith?" Jesus was not able to do many miracles in his hometown because of the unbelief of the people there (Matthew 13:58). Just as faith is required for eternal salvation through Jesus, it is also required for walking in the Lord's promises. Romans 10:17 tells us that faith comes by hearing the Word of God. We want to meditate on and marinate ourselves in His Word. Knowing His Word and promises causes faith to grow, just as that seed in Mark 4:26-29 grows. Faith is believing Jesus' words, "With men this is impossible, but with God all things are possible" (Matthew 19:26). Romans 4:17 says that God calls into existence the things that do not exist!

Paul tells the church in Ephesus that he continually prays for them,

> that the God of our Lord Jesus Christ, the Father of glory, may give you the Spirit of wisdom and of revelation in the knowledge of him, having the eyes of your hearts enlightened, that you may know what is the hope to which he has called you, what are the riches of his glorious inheritance in the saints, and what is the immeasurable greatness of his power toward us who believe, according to the working of his great might that he worked in Christ when he raised him from the dead and seated him at his right hand in the heavenly places, far above all rule and authority and power and dominion, and above every name that is named, not only in this age but also in the one to come. (Ephesians 1:17-21)

Having a better understanding of God's promises, as you bless others by using the gifts God has given you and plant seed for His purposes, you should also set an intention to RECEIVE. God's Word states giving and receiving go together. As I shared earlier, I had to learn how to open my arms to the increase God was providing. Who are we to limit God's blessings?

You may find you need help being a generous giver. You may also find you need some help becoming a grateful receiver. God's will is BOTH. Sometimes a sense of unworthiness can keep us from receiving all God has intended for us. In essence, knowing our sinful past, we try to "pay" again and again by resisting God's grace, generosity, and love to us. Being a good receiver goes back to knowing our identity in Jesus. Remember, the enemy of our soul likes to keep us from realizing our identity. In my experience, he uses lies, shame, and guilt to keep us from walking in our God-given identity. But, in Christ Jesus, we can live in VICTORY instead!

Sometimes, the knowledge that the love of money, selfishness, and greed are sin can keep us from receiving what God wants to give. Remember, God does not bless His children with resources and "seed" for selfish purposes, such as hoarding and greed, but rather so we can be generous conduits of His goodness to the world around us. In His Word, there are passages that teach us how NOT to steward the resources He gives us, such as the parable about the dishonest manager in Luke 16, or the story about the farmer in Luke 12. Both sought their own gain, rather than putting God first. Jesus summarizes the Luke 12 parable with "This is how it will be with whoever stores up things for themselves but is not rich toward God." And, in Luke 16, "And if you are untrustworthy about worldly wealth, who will trust you with the true riches of heaven? And if you are not faithful with other people's things, why should you be trusted with things of your own?" God is looking for those who will steward finances and resources wisely. This takes us back to Module One, where we discussed, above all things, loving God with all our heart, mind, soul, and strength.

As we gratefully receive God's blessings, we are reminded of what He told the nation of Israel in Deuteronomy 8:11-18.

> Take care lest you forget the LORD your God by not keeping his commandments and his rules and his statutes, which I command you today, lest, when you have eaten and are full and have built good houses and live in them, and when your herds and flocks multiply and your silver and gold is multiplied and all that you have is multiplied, then your heart be lifted up, and you forget the LORD your God, who brought you out

of the land of Egypt, out of the house of slavery, who led you through the great and terrifying wilderness, with its fiery serpents and scorpions and thirsty ground where there was no water, who brought you water out of the flinty rock, who fed you in the wilderness with manna that your fathers did not know, that he might humble you and test you, to do you good in the end. Beware lest you say in your heart, 'My power and the might of my hand have gotten me this wealth.' You shall remember the LORD your God, for it is he who gives you power to get wealth, that he may confirm his covenant that he swore to your fathers, as it is this day.

So, as we receive, we praise Him and give Him the glory, knowing that all good things are from Him! Ephesians 3:20-21 says, "Now to him who is able to do far more abundantly than all that we ask or think, according to the power at work within us, to him be glory in the church and in Christ Jesus throughout all generations, forever and ever." This verse helps me remember how infinite God is — it deepens my faith and keeps me wildly excited about what He is doing next and how I can partner with Him!

Finding the Dream Within You

MODULE SIX: FINDING THE DREAM WITHIN YOU.

We have done a lot of work on old emotions and beliefs that belong to the person you were before Jesus redeemed you. These do NOT belong to us as a new creation in Christ. Paul writes in II Corinthians 5:17, "Therefore, if anyone is in Christ, he is a new creation. The old has passed away; behold, the new has come." We are no longer to live as the "old man" (carnal nature) but rather walk in our born-again, redeemed nature. I believe God has put dreams within each of us, intending to equip us to achieve them. As Christians, we can often feel guilty about having big dreams or seemingly outlandish goals.

In the first five modules, we talked about the scriptural basis of being a child of the Most High God and living in His freedom, provision, and promises! We have covered how to allow the Holy Spirit to reveal long-held beliefs or emotions and release them, if we choose. We have talked about our Heavenly Father, who is beyond all we can imagine, and who DESIRES for you to walk in His love, promises, and blessings! But He has given us the gift of free will, so it is up to us to say "yes!"

In this module, I will take you through some exercises to help you discover the dream within you. Instead of feeling ashamed or presumptuous about your dreams, know God puts plans and visions within us! It is important to give them a face and a place so God can fulfill what he has written about us. Psalm 139:16 (NIV) says, "Your eyes saw my unformed body; all the days ordained for me were written in your book before one of them came to be."

> **PSALM 139:16**
> Your eyes saw my unformed body; all the days ordained for me were written in your book before one of them came to be.

God has written a book about you before you were ever born! He has purpose and plans for you! So, when we say "yes" to Him, He helps us fulfill our God-given purpose and calling!

To help you find that dream within you, I invite you to take a quick "photo tour" of your life. Let me explain.

Willie and I have sold quite a few homes in our 22 years of marriage. One thing I always found helpful when selling a home was to take a quick picture of each room. This snapshot gave me an objective look at what needed to be removed and decluttered and what needed to be added. This exposed things I had missed previously.

When you take a picture of a room you are used to living in, the photo reveals things you did not notice in person. We can become so accustomed to how things look now; it can be challenging to imagine how it could be better or to see remedies and solutions that are right in front of us.

Let's take this concept and apply it to our life!

TIME TO IMPLEMENT!

In this exercise, I ask you to take a quick "mental snapshot" of different areas of your life. When you do this, "take" the photos in black and white in your mind. God does not intend for you to stay where you are right now, so we do not want to get too comfy in the "now" reality. He has abundant blessings in store for you!

Close your eyes and take a few minutes to ask the Holy Spirit to guide you in this exercise.

First things first, take a quick "photo" of your spiritual walk with God. Do you feel close to Him? Can you take time to be in His Word each day? Do you include Him in every part of your day? Do you talk with Him about decisions? Do you feel like you are walking through life with your best friend beside you? Do you see room for growth in your relationship with God? Write your thoughts.

_____

_____

_____

_____

_____

Next, snapshot your other relationships, including your marriage (if you are married) and your relationships with your children, grandchildren, family members, church family, friends, and co-workers. Is there joy there? Are there any broken relationships you would love to see redeemed? Do you have people against whom you are holding anger, resentment, bitterness, or unforgiveness?

_____

_____

_____

_____

Now take a quick snapshot of your living space. I want you to look around. Is the kitchen a room you enjoy? Do you like your bedroom? Do you have an office space that suits you? Does your space allow you to feel comfortable and at peace? Are there a few things you wouldn't mind seeing improved?

_____

_____

_____

_____

Next, take a mental picture of your vehicle. How do you feel when you get inside your mode of transportation? Is it a vehicle you enjoy?

_____

_____

_____

_____

It is time to take a snapshot of your daily work or career. Does it reward you well for your time invested? Does it bring you joy? Do you find the work fulfilling? Is this what you see yourself doing long-term? Do you feel a spiritual calling along with the natural purpose in your career?

_____

_____

_____

_____

Next up is your ability to do the things you would like to do. For example, can you travel where and when you would like? Are you able to visit loved ones who don't live near you? Can you say yes when your kids want to take karate or ballet lessons, or would like to play traveling baseball? Are you able to say yes to the experiences you want for yourself and your loved ones?

_____

_____

_____

_____

_____

Snapshot your health. Do you have the energy to do what God calls you to do? Is your body in a state of health, or are you facing some health challenges? Are you as fit as you would like? Is the food you are eating supporting your body's wellness?

_____

_____

_____

_____

How about your bank account? Is it how you would like it? Are there too many auto-pay bills going out and not enough deposits arriving? Is it providing resources for your heart's desire to help others and contribute to meaningful causes? Are you able to be generous in all situations?

_____

_____

_____

_____

_____

It is good to assess areas of your life where you see room for growth and improvement, but now, I'm going to let you put those black-and-white mental photos aside. Of course, they will always be part of your before-story, which God will use to bless others in their journey. But now **it is time to move FORWARD**.

It is time for your RESET! God is not the source of lack, poverty, scarcity, or pain. Instead, He desires to do and give abundantly more than you can think, ask, or imagine!! Here is your moment to think about things from a "Wouldn't it be so amazing if..." perspective. Those dreams are not in your heart by accident. It is time to give them space to grow.

NOW is the time to believe in God's absolutely-abundantly-beyond-anything-you-could-even- think-ask-or-imagine blessings! In Christ, we get to have our story rewritten! Not only do we get "a ticket to heaven" when we believe and receive Jesus as our Lord and Savior, but also, God desires to move in us to help us RESET our life to live in His promises, provision, love, joy, and peace!

Take time to assess what you would LIKE to see in each of these areas of your life! What do you want to speak over each part? Say these things boldly! Do not be shy in asking God for the desires of your heart! He has given us a new heart under the new covenant through Jesus, and in that new heart, He has put dreams, goals, and plans for our future. Speak BLESSING over all areas of your life. Speak these things as if they are already happening.

Spiritually speaking, what do you want in your relationship with God? Please write it down! Think of walking with Him at a different level; what emotions do you feel? Would you experience intense joy? Would you notice your peace overflowing? Would you find you can't even explain why and how you are so joyful?

_____

_____

_____

_____

_____

Now as you think about your relationships, what do they look like if you are living in God's unlimited ability and provision? How does your marriage look? If you are not yet married, what qualities do you see in your future spouse? What do you see for your children and relationships with them? Ask yourself the same questions regarding friendships, work relationships, and connections with other family members. I invite you to feel the emotions of love and joy inside your heart because of thriving relationships. Imagine broken relationships healed and restored.

_____

_____

_____

_____

_____

How do you want your dwelling space to look? What will this enhanced space allow? Might you choose to have people over more often? Does it give you more room for something you enjoy? Do you need to hire help to create and keep your space? What about this NEW picture brings you joy? I want you to FEEL the emotions of this new space!! WRITE these things down in the present tense, as if they are already your reality! Remember the lesson found in Mark 11:24. Write these things believing you have already received them.

_____

_____

How would you like your travel, experiences, and activities to look? Would you like them to be no longer limited by time or money? What does it feel like when you can take the trips you have dreamed of, do the mission work you are drawn to, or allow children opportunity for certain activities or experiences?

How about your work or career? If you were able to do something you love and earn a meaningful income from it, what would it be? Imagine how you would feel walking in the gifts God gave you within your career or calling. What emotions are you feeling in this space? WRITE DOWN your desires as if they have already happened!

As we move to your bank account, picture the income deposited and the automatic withdrawals to give to your church, missions, or causes you are passionate about, as well as bills or debts you would like to pay in full. What feeling do you have as you look at your abundant bank account and ability to live free from debt while giving more generously than you ever imagined? Jot down how you feel about this new reality.

_____

_____

_____

_____

_____

WRITING DOWN the dreams and visions He has put within you is powerful. Our handwriting has a special connection to our brain, so this is a moment when writing out your vision, hopes, and dreams is preferable over typing. Write in the present tense or as if it were already reality (Mark 11:24). One way to do this is to pretend you are looking **back** over the current year telling all the amazing things that happened. Here's an example of how it might look:

"Wow! I can't even believe all that has happened this past year! Our business has doubled, and we now have $[_____] in the bank. I have been giving [___] % of my income to our church and have an auto-deposit going to [my favorite charity] each month. I am seeing and receiving God's increase of the seeds we are sowing. We were able to pay off our car and mortgage in full, and now we are [example of anything else the added money allows]. We were able to pay for the [specific vehicle] in cash! Last year, we were able to put the kids into [specific school] and start a college fund. We are planning our mission trip to [_____] next year. Our marriage is better than ever, with us both seeking the Lord first every day, having prayer time together, and fitting in weekly date nights! Thank you, Lord, for your gracious, loving blessings to us! We look forward to the year ahead!"

First, always ask for the Holy Spirit's guidance. Then, grab your pen, and start writing! This is a no-judgment zone. Just write. Speak and write blessings over you, your loved ones, and the various areas of your life.

_____

_____

_____

_____

_____

_____

_____

Next, cut out photos to represent each part of your vision, goals, and dreams and paste them on paper. Or, even easier, use your computer to "paste" photos into a document. Then have the completed version PRINTED in color.

Sometimes this is called a vision board or dream board. Vision is important. If you don't know where you're going, you will likely not get "there." In Hosea 4:6, it says, "My people are destroyed for lack of knowledge." God wants us to spend time seeking HIS clarity on our vision and gaining the knowledge we need to bring it into being. He is our teacher and guide along the way.

The last step is to pray through the small steps God wants you to take to begin bringing this vision, dream, and purpose into being. Psalm 32:8 (NIV) says, "I will instruct you and teach you in the way you should go; I will counsel you with my loving eye on you." Wow, such a beautiful blessing! God DOES want you to take action! I love these two verses in Proverbs 16. In verse 3, "Commit your work to the LORD, and your plans will be established." And in verse 9, "The heart of man plans his way, but the LORD establishes his steps." God loves to partner with us on which actions we are to take next, but He does ask that we act.

And again, God created man in His image, so our words are creative! Speak a blessing over these things. Speak out what you WANT instead of what you do not want.

Each morning, ask the Lord, "Lord, what actions do You want me to take today?" Then as He brings an idea, WRITE it down right then and determine in your heart to implement it that day. Do not procrastinate in your actions when He prompts, or you may be slowing down the process of bringing His intended blessings into your life! He will lead you the entire way!

For example, He may sometimes prompt you to search for something online or to phone a certain friend. He may bring someone into your life who shares a message in perfect timing for you. In my experience, He has often used others to speak and confirm what He is saying or to lead me into my next steps. He is so patient with us and knows we may sometimes need to hear it more than once! It also thrills me how He uses us in each other's lives! Sometimes YOU will be the person with the word someone else needs to hear. Sometimes someone else will be the one bringing you the word in season.

When we partner with God, it is an incredible thrill and joy how He interweaves our journeys together! When you feel a prompting from the Holy Spirit, I encourage you not to put it off. First, double check it is aligned with the Bible. Scripture is always our first filter to make sure that a message is from God! Become an avid student of God's Word! Then, if scripturally aligned, take action.

ACTION Time.

MODULE SEVEN: ACTION TIME.

I am an action girl. I like to jump in and "do." So "waiting on the Lord" and being patient has not always been my strong suit. I have learned that action is always best done after first seeking the Lord.

When the Holy Spirit prompts us, God loves to see us implement and act on what He has shown us. So, as we dive into the "action" side of things, first implement these ABCs:

A: Assess in prayer and scripture.
B: Believe God's promises are true.
C: Confidently walk in His promises (otherwise known as faith).

I hope you are already feeling the freedom of dropping the old faulty mindsets, beliefs, and emotions at the foot of the cross, and having God replace them with His truth found in the Bible! Hopefully, you feel CONFIDENT in your identity in Christ Jesus as a child of God.

It is time to give God spaces and places to bless you. Now is when we APPLY our knowledge. God loves to guide us! He loves it when we walk in obedience to His leading and prompting! The Bible tells us those who are faithful over little will receive more (Matthew 25:21). When we are faithful to say "Yes, Lord!", He continues giving us more and more.

Remember, when we give God the reins of our life, He leads us into obedience (I John 5:2-3) and the desire to say "yes" to Him! In Christ, we become motivated by love for Him. He is not only our Savior but also our Lord! So, to live in His bountiful provision, we need to be quick to say "yes" when He moves or prompts us. My motto is "Be quick with my yes!" I do not want to slow down, through my procrastination, the blessings He has planned!

> **Lord, THANK YOU for the dreams and hopes You have put within me. Cause me to walk them out in the strength You give me! Lead me each step of the way. As You guide me, I say "yes!" In the mighty name of Jesus let these things be so! Lord, let me fulfill the purpose and calling for which You have created me! Let my life glorify You!**

In my life, God has used opportunities, ideas, inspirations, concepts, and other people to bring blessings. For example, I remember a time when I was praying for an executive assistant who would be the right fit for my business. I am not kidding when I tell you I was praying God would inspire her to walk up to my door asking for the position.

I waited for three and a half years. Do you know what I did not do? I did not take any action that would make it easy for God to bring that right person. Finally, one day, I decided to post on our neighborhood group, saying I was looking for an assistant and what the job would include. Within that day, I had two fabulous assistants added to my executive team!

What is the moral of this story? When we take God-inspired ACTION in faith, it gives God more avenues to bring blessing!

It is helpful to determine precisely how much money it will cost to fulfill the dreams you wrote down. For instance, if you want to pay the mortgage in full, do research to see exactly how much you owe. If you need a different vehicle, find the one you think would be the best fit for you, and figure out what it will cost. Are you feeling moved to plan a specific trip? Again, find out how much it will cost.

Once you know how much will be needed to make your vision a reality, remember it is often the small steps in faith that will bring you there. Here is where GOALS come in! Writing intentional, achievable, time-sensitive goals can help you take the small daily, weekly, and monthly action steps needed to get you to your larger dream and vision. The key here is praying each morning and asking God to lay on your heart which actions He wants you to take next.

You can open your day with, "Good morning, Lord! I love you! What is it You have for me to do today? Give me the strength, knowledge, and wisdom to complete it today." Remember, His strength is new each day. Lamentations 3:22-23 says, "The steadfast love of the LORD never ceases; his mercies never come to an end; they are new every morning; great is your faithfulness." Our God NEVER runs out of things to give us when we come to Him and ask. He is the Creator and God of the universe. The only thing limiting Him is the free will He has given us. May we willingly seek His guidance, believe it is His will to bless us, and say "yes" to walking it out.

> **LAMENTATIONS 3:22-23**
> The steadfast love of the Lord never ceases; his mercies never come to an end; they are new every morning; great is your faithfulness.

Another crucial action is to implement new belief patterns. Beliefs are simply a well-developed habit. We have "practiced" them repeatedly, creating a well-worn thought path in our brains.

The exciting thing is that these pathways can be rewritten into NEW, true, beneficial thought habits. Here are some simple starting steps to take.

TIME TO IMPLEMENT!

Ask yourself who you can bless today. What are some gifts you have with which to serve people? Then ACT on what God lays on your heart!

It is often a small "yes" which leads you into the vision and dream He has given you. When God gives you a prompting or idea, even if it seems small, practice saying "yes" and implementing it.

Practice agreeing with and speaking God's truth and blessing over your life, finances, job, community, and loved ones. Remember, thoughts are like habits, whether good or bad. Speaking these blessings will become your new way of thinking. Ask the Holy Spirit's help in bringing these new truths to your remembrance!

Stop feeding the old thoughts, beliefs, and emotions. Do not let old thought habits drag you back. You are a new creation in Christ! You now walk in His freedom and victory!!

Talk with God often, asking Him to give you His direction on the next action He calls you to take. Then, commit in your heart to step into that action in faith.

MY PRAYER OF BLESSING FOR YOU

I thank God for His love and favor upon you! As His beloved child, may you walk in His promises all your days! I pray your faith will continually grow and that you will confidently place your finances and possessions under God's direction and jurisdiction. May you give cheerfully and abundantly, knowing you cannot outgive God! Open your arms to receive His all-powerful love, grace, joy, and abundant life. With the Holy Spirit dwelling in you, may the fruit of His Spirit abound! I bless you to become a student of His Holy Bible, with the Holy Spirit as your teacher, growing a deeper and deeper love and craving more and more time with Him. May you hear His voice and feel His presence throughout your days. May you diligently seek His face, learn His will, and walk in His statutes, empowered by the Holy Spirit. May "Yes, Lord!" be your heart-cry, as He leads you! May you thrive and grow in Christ Jesus! In Jesus' Mighty Name I pray!

R-E-S-E-T

REST IN HIM
EQUIP YOURSELF WITH HIS WORD
SET YOUR EYES ON JESUS
EXPECT HIS PROMISES TO BE YES & AMEN
TAKE THE DAILY ACTIONS HE GIVES YOU

PERSONAL NOTES

I have found sometimes as I seek God's help and guidance, He gives me the big 20,000-foot-high view and vision. At other times, He asks me to take one small step in faith without seeing the entire vision. Sometimes, I may not know the "why" behind His ask, but I trust Him completely and know He works all things together for my good, as Romans 8:28 tells us. God loves our trusting obedience to walk and partner with Him.

Early in my marriage, God began working on my heart to be quick with my "Yes, Lord!" I desired to align with Him in every area of my life. I remember asking Him two things: "Lord, I am willing…lead me gently," and "Lord, lead Willie and me together." Over the years, Willie and I have had several times where God spoke to one or both of us. We had the opportunity to say "Yes, Lord!" When we did, there was blessing.

One such time was when we felt called to move to Texas. We had built a beautiful, comfortable life in South Dakota. We were near our family and friends. I felt the calling urgently and clearly. God was calling us to Texas. When Willie asked if I felt we were to move because of our direct-selling business, my answer was clear: No. I felt God very specifically saying He was calling us to move for "family" reasons.

Willie kindly reminded me that most of our family lived in the Midwest, NOT in Texas. He was 100% correct. Yet, the message was strong and clear. Move for family.

In a very short amount of time, we said "Yes." We drove to the area we felt God calling us and purchased a home over the timespan of a weekend. At the time of this writing, we have been in Texas for five years. In some ways, these have been the most difficult five years of my life, but through it all, God has been so faithful to work things together for good. We have not fully seen the reasons He called us here, but He has already brought my sister and her beautiful family to our same area. In addition, both Willie's sister and his brother and their families are also within just a few hours of us. Our two oldest sons are attending Texas A&M. We moved knowing very little about the "why," but being fully convinced we were to step out in faith.

While the ways people hear God differs, I have found that I often hear God's voice in my own thoughts. There is a knowing in my spirit that the thought was not my own. It is often an answer to prayer, a message or command, or a random idea that feels like an amazing gift. It is like having a thought-conversation between my human thoughts and God's promptings. Sometimes I feel His voice deeply in my heart. It is not audible, but almost so clear I would wonder if it were!

God can speak in infinite ways! So, look for His voice and hand in every area of your life, and watch what starts to happen! He is speaking to us all the time! It could be through a particular song, someone else in your life, something in nature, numbers, and more! He is God! He is not limited in how He can talk with you! So, if you're waiting to hear from Him, ask Him to show you where He is ALREADY speaking to you… because He is.

For example, I remember being at the ranch (prior to writing this book) and having an emotional moment of frustration and doubt. "Lord, I want MORE of you! I want to hear you MORE clearly and MORE often. I want to KNOW You more!"

Now, this may sound presumptuous to say to the Creator of the universe, but when it comes to seeking MORE of Him, it thrills His heart, too. In that moment, He brought the lyrics of an old hymn into my mind, "And He walks with me, and He talks with me, and He tells me I am His own! And the joy we share, as we tarry there, none other has ever known."

But He asked me, instead, to sing it TO Him, changing the words to, "And You walk with me, and You talk with me! And You tell me I am Your own! And the joy we SHARE, as we tarry here, is like none other I've ever known."

What blew me away was this. I heard the Lord say, "The joy is not only yours when we spend time together. It is equally my joy to spend time with you!" Wow! It brought me to tears, sobbing in gratitude and immense love, realizing He loves to spend time with us, too. It is not a one-sided relationship. We bring JOY to His heart by spending time with Him!

So, when I hear a prompting, an idea, or a command in thought, I ask Him to empower me to act on it. "Yes, Lord!" has been my heart-cry in recent years. "For we are God's masterpiece. He has created us anew in Christ Jesus, so we can do the good things he planned for us long ago" (Ephesians 2:10 NLT).

When God gives an idea, thought, or direction, thank Him for it. Then ask Him to give you the strength and ability to walk it out, according to His promise in Ezekiel 36:27: "And I will put my Spirit within you, and cause you to walk in my statutes and be careful to obey my rules."

EZEKIEL 36:27

And I will put my Spirit within you, and cause you to walk in my statutes and be careful to obey my rules.

With the Holy Spirit's continued guidance, action is always best taken in God's strength, not our own. II Corinthians 9:8 says, "And God is able to make all grace abound to you, so that having all sufficiency in all things at all times, you may abound in every good work." Did you highlight ALL of times "all" appeared in the passage?!

As a believer, you have access to the limitlessness of God—His creativity, strength, and motivation. Believe for supernatural provision all along the journey. Then, when you look for His supernatural provision, you will be blown away!

We have many examples in the Bible of Jesus' miracles, like when Jesus turned water into wine or when he multiplied the loaves and fishes. When Jesus fed the 4,000 and the 5,000 men (not counting the women and children), he first asked his disciples what they had. What they had to offer seemed insufficient, insignificant, and inadequate. But **Jesus took their "little" and blessed it to multiply the results and impact**. Remember, when you come to the Lord seeking a miracle, He asks us to bring our "little" so He can bless it and bring the miraculous multiplication! What seed are you sowing? He can multiply it!

Consider the words of Jesus in one of my favorite verses, John 14:12, "Truly, truly, I say to you, whoever believes in me will also do the works that I do; and greater works than these will he do, because I am going to the Father."

More incredible things than Jesus did when He walked as a man here on Earth?! Yes. That is what the Word says.

And you know what is extra awesome?! John 8:36 says, "So if the Son sets you free, you will be free indeed." In Galatians 5:1, Paul wrote, "For freedom Christ has set us free; stand firm therefore, and do not submit again to a yoke of slavery." Freedom in Christ is all-encompassing to me, but since we are talking about a money mindset, it also includes freedom from debt and bondage! Remember, Jesus comes that we may have life and have it abundantly (John 10:10).

John 15:7 says, "If you abide in me, and my words abide in you, ask whatever you wish, and it will be done for you." So, by abiding IN CHRIST and His Holy Spirit in us, we ask whatever we wish, and it will be done. John 16:23 says, "Truly, truly, I say to you, whatever you ask of the Father in my name, he will give it to you."

There are so many beautiful promises throughout the Bible. As a born-again child of God, you are grafted into these promises! Hallelujah! Thank you, Jesus!

In Philippians 4:6, Paul writes, "Do not be anxious about anything, but in everything by prayer and supplication with thanksgiving let your requests be made known to God." He is reminding us that God loves our prayers and requests. And the thing about God is that He loves to answer our prayers in ways that are far above and beyond what we can think or even ask, according to the power of His Holy Spirit in us! He loves to exceed our expectations (Ephesians 3:20-21)!

I am excited to hear about your transformations as you live in your true identity and speak and receive God's blessing over your life. Let's agree on this: God has no difficulty granting your desires. He knows exactly what you need, and He created you with dreams, a purpose, and a calling. He wants to give you the desires of your heart (Psalm 37:4)!

In resetting your financial mindset, seek His kingdom and righteousness first; then, the other things will be covered! He is a covenant-keeping God. He will cause you, through the power of His

Holy Spirit in you, to fulfill your part when you make Him Lord of your life. We only need to say yes to Him and give Him the throne of our life. And you do not have to worry about how He will do these things. Believe and know it is done because He is God of His Word! He loves your ask! He loves your diligence in coming to Him! **He loves YOU!** As you shift your financial mindset, serve Him. Talk with Him. Pray for others. Use your spiritual gifts. Tell others about Jesus, the One who set you free!

> **NUMBERS 6:24-26**
>
> The LORD bless you and keep you; the LORD make his face to shine upon you and be gracious to you; the LORD lift up his countenance upon you and give you peace.

Appendix A

I have taken a few scriptures and put each into a prayer format for you to speak over your life and the lives of your loved ones. These are just a few examples of how I speak God's Word over myself and my loved ones. You can do this with many other verses throughout the Bible. You can pray these promises over your life because we, as believers, are in Christ Jesus!

Ephesians 1:16-21 "I do not cease to give thanks for you, remembering you in my prayers, that the God of our Lord Jesus Christ, the Father of glory, may give you the Spirit of wisdom and of revelation in the knowledge of him, having the eyes of your hearts enlightened, that you may know what is the hope to which he has called you, what are the riches of his glorious inheritance in the saints, and what is the immeasurable greatness of his power toward us who believe, according to the working of his great might that he worked in Christ when he raised him from the dead and seated him at his right hand in the heavenly places, far above all rule and authority and power and dominion, and above every name that is named, not only in this age but also in the one to come."

> Thank You, Father God, for giving me spiritual wisdom and revelation so I might grow in my knowledge of You. Enlighten the eyes of my heart so I can understand the confident hope You have given me and the riches of Your glorious inheritance. Thank You for revealing the incredible greatness of Your power for us who believe. This same mighty power raised Christ from the dead and seated him at Your right hand, far above any ruler, authority, power, leader, or anything else in this world and the world to come.

Philippians 4:19 "And my God will supply every need of yours according to his riches in glory in Christ Jesus."

> You, oh God, will supply my every need according to Your abundant riches in glory in Christ Jesus.

Colossians 1:9-14 "And so, from the day we heard, we have not ceased to pray for you, asking that you may be filled with the knowledge of his will in all spiritual wisdom and understanding, so as to walk in a manner worthy of the Lord, fully pleasing to him: bearing fruit in every good work and increasing in the knowledge of God; being strengthened with all power, according to his glorious might, for all endurance and patience with joy; giving thanks to the Father, who has qualified you to share in the inheritance of the saints in light. He has delivered us from the domain of darkness and transferred us to the kingdom of his beloved Son, in whom we have redemption, the forgiveness of sins."

> God, thank You for filling me with the knowledge of Your will through the wisdom and understanding that the Holy Spirit gives, that I may live a life worthy of You and please You in every way: bearing fruit in every good work, growing in the knowledge of You, and being strengthened with ALL power according to Your glorious might! You, Father, have qualified me to share in the inheritance of Your people in the kingdom of light. Thank you for rescuing me from the dominion of darkness and bringing me into the kingdom of Your Son, in whom I have redemption!

Deuteronomy 28:12 "The Lord will open to you his good treasury, the heavens, to give the rain to your land in its season and to bless all the work of your hands. And you shall lend to many nations, but you shall not borrow."

> Lord, open to us Your good treasury, the heavens, to give rain to our land in season and to bless the work of our hands. Let us lend but have no need to borrow.

Psalm 20:4-7 (NIV) "May he give you the desire of your heart and make all your plans succeed. May we shout for joy over your victory and lift up our banners in the name of our God. May the LORD grant all your requests. Now this I know: The LORD gives victory to his anointed. He answers him from his heavenly sanctuary with the victorious power of his right hand. Some trust in chariots and some in horses, but we trust in the name of the LORD our God."

> Lord, thank you for giving us the desire of our hearts and making our plans succeed. May we ever shout for joy over Your victory and lift up our banners in Your name, oh Lord! May you grant us our requests. This I know: You, oh Lord, give victory to Your anointed. You answer us from Your heavenly sanctuary with the victorious power of Your right hand. Some trust in chariots and some in horses, but we trust in Your name, Lord God!

Psalm 23 (NIV) "The LORD is my shepherd, I lack nothing. He makes me lie down in green pastures, he leads me beside quiet waters, he refreshes my soul. He guides me along the right paths for his name's sake. Even though I walk through the darkest valley, I will fear no evil, for you are with me; your rod and your staff, they comfort me. You prepare a table before me in the presence of my enemies. You anoint my head with oil; my cup overflows. Surely your goodness and love will follow me all the days of my life, and I will dwell in the house of the LORD forever."

> You, oh Lord, are my shepherd, I lack nothing. You make me lie down in green pastures, You lead me beside quiet waters. You refresh my soul! You guide me along the right paths for Your name's sake. Even though I walk through the darkest valley, I fear no evil for You are with me; Your rod and Your staff comfort me. You prepare a table before me in the presence of my enemies. You anoint my head with oil, my cup overflows. Surely Your goodness and love will follow me all the days of my life, and I dwell in Your house, oh Lord, forever!

Psalm 37:3-5 "Trust in the LORD, and do good; dwell in the land and befriend faithfulness. Delight yourself in the LORD, and he will give you the desires of your heart. Commit your way to the LORD; trust in him, and he will act."

> I trust in You, Lord, and choose to do good; I dwell in the land and befriend faithfulness. I delight myself in You, Lord, and You give me the desires of my heart. I commit my way to You, oh Lord; I trust You and know You will act!

Psalm 62:10 "Put no trust in extortion; set no vain hopes on robbery; if riches increase, set not your heart on them."

> I put no trust in extortion; I set no hopes on robbery; as riches increase, I will not set my heart on them. In Your strength and wisdom, I will be a good steward of all that you give, remembering to above all, love You with all of my heart, mind, soul, and strength.

Psalm 90:17 "Let the favor of the Lord our God be upon us, and establish the work of our hands upon us; yes, establish the work of our hands!"

> Lord God, let Your favor be upon us and establish the work of our hands!

Psalm 103:2-5 "Bless the LORD, O my soul, and forget not all his benefits, who forgives all your iniquity, who heals all your diseases, who redeems your life from the pit, who crowns you with steadfast love and mercy, who satisfies you with good so that your youth is renewed like the eagle's."

> **Bless You, oh Lord! I will not forget Your benefits, You who forgives all my iniquity, heals our diseases, redeemed our life from the pit, who crowns us with steadfast love and mercy, who satisfies us with good so that our youth is renewed like the eagle's.**

Psalm 112:1-3 "Blessed is the man who fears the LORD, who greatly delights in his commandments! His offspring will be mighty in the land; the generation of the upright will be blessed. Wealth and riches are in his house, and his righteousness endures forever."

> **Blessed is the one who fears You, Lord, who delights in Your commandments! Your word tells us their offspring will be mighty in the land; the generation of the upright will be blessed. Wealth and riches are in their house and their righteousness endures forever.**
> **I love You and delight in Your commandments and receive this promise and blessing in Christ Jesus!!**

Psalm 145:18-20 "The LORD is near to all who call on him, to all who call on him in truth. He fulfills the desire of those who fear him; he also hears their cry and saves them. The LORD preserves all who love him, but all the wicked he will destroy."

> **Lord, You are near to ALL who call on You in truth! You fulfill the desires of those who fear You! You hear our cry and save us. You preserve all who love You!**
> **I love You, Lord!**

Proverbs 10:22 "The blessing of the Lord makes rich, and he adds no sorrow with it."

> **Lord, Your blessing makes us rich and You add no sorrow with it!**

Ezekiel 36:26-28 "And I will give you a new heart, and a new spirit I will put within you. And I will remove the heart of stone from your flesh and give you a heart of flesh. And I will put my Spirit within you, and cause you to walk in my statutes and be careful to obey my rules. You shall dwell in the land that I gave to your fathers, and you shall be my people, and I will be your God."

> **Thank You for giving me a new heart and a new spirit in Christ Jesus! Thank You for putting Your Spirit in me and causing me to walk in Your statutes and obey Your commands.**

Appendix B

I am including a few more passages to read as you continue to seek Him and dive into His Word. Each day, before you open your Bible, invite the Holy Spirit to walk with you through the scriptures. It is always best to, as one of my friends says, "Read the Bible WITH the Author!"

I am praying God's blessings upon you! God is excited for your "yes," as you continue your journey with Him!

Leviticus 26:3-13 "If you walk in my statutes and observe my commandments and do them, then I will give you your rains in their season, and the land shall yield its increase, and the trees of the field shall yield their fruit. Your threshing shall last to the time of the grape harvest, and the grape harvest shall last to the time for sowing. And you shall eat your bread to the full and dwell in your land securely. I will give peace in the land, and you shall lie down, and none shall make you afraid. And I will remove harmful beasts from the land, and the sword shall not go through your land. You shall chase your enemies, and they shall fall before you by the sword. Five of you shall chase a hundred, and a hundred of you shall chase ten thousand, and your enemies shall fall before you by the sword. I will turn to you and make you fruitful and multiply you and will confirm my covenant with you. You shall eat old store long kept, and you shall clear out the old to make way for the new. I will make my dwelling among you, and my soul shall not abhor you. And I will walk among you and will be your God, and you shall be my people. I am the LORD your God, who brought you out of the land of Egypt, that you should not be their slaves. And I have broken the bars of your yoke and made you walk erect."

Deuteronomy 8:17-18 (NLT) "He did all this so you would never say to yourself, 'I have achieved this wealth with my own strength and energy.' Remember the Lord your God. He is the one who gives you power to be successful, in order to fulfill the covenant he confirmed to your ancestors with an oath."

Deuteronomy 28:1-14 "And if you faithfully obey the voice of the LORD your God, being careful to do all his commandments that I command you today, the LORD your God will set you high above all the nations of the earth. And all these blessings shall come upon you and overtake you, if you obey the voice of the LORD your God. Blessed shall you be in the city, and blessed shall you be in the field. Blessed shall be the fruit of your womb and the fruit of your ground and the fruit of your cattle, the increase of your herds and the young of your flock. Blessed shall be your basket and your kneading bowl. Blessed shall you be when you come in, and blessed shall you be when you go out. The LORD will cause your enemies who rise against you to be defeated before you. They shall come out against you one way and flee before you seven ways. The LORD will command the blessing on you in your barns and in all that you undertake. And he will bless you in the land that the LORD your God is giving you. The LORD will establish you as a people holy to himself, as he has sworn to you, if you keep the commandments of the LORD your God and walk in his ways. And all the peoples of the earth shall see that you are called by the name of the LORD, and they shall be afraid of you. And the LORD will make you abound in prosperity, in the fruit of your womb and in the fruit of your livestock and in the fruit of your ground, within the land that the LORD swore to your fathers to give you. The LORD will open to you his good treasury, the heavens, to give the rain to your land in its season and to bless all the work of your hands. And you shall lend to many nations, but you shall not borrow. And the LORD will make you the head and not the tail, and you shall only go up and not down, if you obey the commandments of the LORD your God, which I command you today, being careful to do them, and if you do not turn aside from any of the words that I command you today, to the right hand or to the left, to go after other gods to serve them."

I Chronicles 29:11-12 "Yours, O LORD, is the greatness and the power and the glory and the victory and the majesty, for all that is in the heavens and in the earth is yours. Yours is the kingdom, O LORD, and you are exalted as head above all. Both riches and honor come from you, and you rule over all. In your hand are power and might, and in your hand it is to make great and to give strength to all."

Psalm 91 (NIV) "Whoever dwells in the shelter of the Most High will rest in the shadow of the Almighty. I will say of the LORD, 'He is my refuge and my fortress, my God, in whom I trust.' Surely he will save you from the fowler's snare and from the deadly pestilence. He will cover you with his feathers, and under his wings you will find refuge; his faithfulness will be your shield and rampart. You will not fear the terror of night, nor the arrow that flies by day, nor the pestilence that stalks in the darkness, nor the plague that destroys at midday. A thousand may fall at your side, ten thousand at your right hand, but it will not come near you. You will only observe with your eyes and see the punishment of the wicked. If you say, 'The LORD is my refuge,' and you make the Most High your dwelling, no harm will overtake you, no disaster will come near your tent. For he will command his angels concerning you to guard you in all your ways;

they will lift you up in their hands, so that you will not strike your foot against a stone. You will tread on the lion and the cobra; you will trample the great lion and the serpent. 'Because he loves me,' says the LORD, 'I will rescue him; I will protect him, for he acknowledges my name. He will call on me, and I will answer him; I will be with him in trouble, I will deliver him and honor him. With long life I will satisfy him and show him my salvation.'"

Psalm 103 "Bless the LORD, O my soul, and all that is within me, bless his holy name! Bless the LORD, O my soul, and forget not all his benefits, who forgives all your iniquity, who heals all your diseases, who redeems your life from the pit, who crowns you with steadfast love and mercy, who satisfies you with good so that your youth is renewed like the eagle's. The LORD works righteousness and justice for all who are oppressed. He made known his ways to Moses, his acts to the people of Israel. The LORD is merciful and gracious, slow to anger and abounding in steadfast love. He will not always chide, nor will he keep his anger forever. He does not deal with us according to our sins, nor repay us according to our iniquities. For as high as the heavens are above the earth, so great is his steadfast love toward those who fear him; as far as the east is from the west, so far does he remove our transgressions from us. As a father shows compassion to his children, so the LORD shows compassion to those who fear him. For he knows our frame; he remembers that we are dust. As for man, his days are like grass; he flourishes like a flower of the field; for the wind passes over it, and it is gone, and its place knows it no more. But the steadfast love of the LORD is from everlasting to everlasting on those who fear him, and his righteousness to children's children, to those who keep his covenant and remember to do his commandments. The LORD has established his throne in the heavens, and his kingdom rules over all. Bless the LORD, O you his angels, you mighty ones who do his word, obeying the voice of his word! Bless the LORD, all his hosts, his ministers, who do his will! Bless the LORD, all his works, in all places of his dominion. Bless the LORD, O my soul!"

Psalm 115:14-15 "May the LORD give you increase, you and your children! May you be blessed by the LORD, who made heaven and earth."

Psalm 126 "When the LORD restored the fortunes of Zion, we were like those who dream. Then our mouth was filled with laughter, and our tongue with shouts of joy; then they said among the nations, 'The LORD has done great things for them.' The LORD has done great things for us; we are glad. Restore our fortunes, O LORD, like streams in the Negeb! Those who sow in tears shall reap with shouts of joy! He who goes out weeping, bearing the seed for sowing, shall come home with shouts of joy, bringing his sheaves with him."

Psalm 128:1-2 "Blessed is everyone who fears the LORD, who walks in his ways! You shall eat the fruit of the labor of your hands; you shall be blessed, and it shall be well with you."

Psalm 143:8-10 (NLT) "Let me hear of your unfailing love each morning, for I am trusting you. Show me where to walk, for I give myself to you. Rescue me from my enemies, LORD; I run to you to hide me. Teach me to do your will, for you are my God. May your gracious Spirit lead me forward on a firm footing."

Isaiah 55 (NIV) "Come, all you who are thirsty, come to the waters; and you who have no money, come, buy and eat! Come, buy wine and milk without money and without cost. Why spend money on what is not bread, and your labor on what does not satisfy? Listen, listen to me, and eat what is good, and you will delight in the richest of fare. Give ear and come to me; listen, that you may live. I will make an everlasting covenant with you, my faithful love promised to

David. See, I have made him a witness to the peoples, a ruler and commander of the peoples. Surely you will summon nations you know not, and nations you do not know will come running to you because of the LORD your God, the Holy One of Israel, for he has endowed you with splendor." Seek the LORD while he may be found; call on him while he is near. Let the wicked forsake their ways and the unrighteous their thoughts. Let them turn to the LORD, and he will have mercy on them, and to our God, for he will freely pardon. "For my thoughts are not your thoughts, neither are your ways my ways, declares the LORD. "As the heavens are higher than the earth, so are my ways higher than your ways and my thoughts than your thoughts. As the rain and the snow come down from heaven, and do not return to it without watering the earth and making it bud and flourish, so that it yields seed for the sower and bread for the eater, so is my word that goes out from my mouth: It will not return to me empty, but will accomplish what I desire and achieve the purpose for which I sent it. You will go out in joy and be led forth in peace; the mountains and hills will burst into song before you, and all the trees of the field will clap their hands. Instead of the thornbush will grow the juniper, and instead of briers the myrtle will grow. This will be for the LORD's renown, for an everlasting sign, that will endure forever."

About the Author

Sonya Eckel is passionate about helping others grow and shine in all areas of life! She grew up in a conservative Christian home on a farm in South Dakota. She and her husband, Willie, have been married for over 22 years and she has been a work-from-home mom to their four boys. Her love for the land runs deep, and she and her family enjoy a small wildlife ranch in Texas with chickens, oryx, blackbuck, their sweet Aussiedoodle, Maple, and most recently, geese!

She has loved Jesus for as long as she can remember. In her book, she shares how God has continued to lead her in growing her understanding of Him and His Word. She has found that the more she studies the Bible, the more she discovers God's love for His children!

Her work as a physical therapist, a natural birthing instructor and coach, and most recently, a top leader within the direct sales industry, has allowed her to impact many lives. She has a passion for helping others grow spiritually, as well as in their businesses and life pursuits. She loves helping others live free, in Christ, enjoying the promises and provision that God graciously extends. During her past 14 years in direct sales, she has been recognized for building an incredibly successful team of thousands of consultants, whom she empowers to implement skills and strategies that she has learned on her journey.

Her passion for Jesus shines through in all she does. She helps others walk in their God-given purpose and destiny, teaching how to lean into biblically guided living in order to walk in God's promises.

Sonya can be found on YouTube at https://youtube.com/sonyaeckel and on Instagram at http://instagram.walkinginhispromises.com/. She also enjoys connecting with her readers in her Facebook community, http://FBCommunity.WalkingInHisPromises.com. Visit her website, www.WalkingInHisPromises.com, for free resources and support on your journey! To download 10 powerful prayers based on the prayers in this book, go to http://PowerfulPrayers.WalkingInHisPromises.com.